CHICAGO PUBLIC LIBRARY

Changing Course

Changing Course

*One Woman's True-Life Adventures
as a Merchant Marine*

Jeanne Lutz

New Horizon Press
Far Hills, New Jersey

New Horizon Press
P.O. Box 669
Far Hills, NJ 07931

Jeanne Lutz
    Changing Course: One Woman's True-Life Adventures as
    a Merchant Marine

Cover Design: Mike Stromberg, The Great American Art Co.
Interior Design: Susan M. Sanderson

Library of Congress Control Number: 2002112730

ISBN: 0-88282-232-2
New Horizon Press

Manufactured in the U.S.A.

2007   2006   2005   2004   2003   /   5   4   3   2   1

Dedication

For professor John Keeble,
with admiration and gratitude

Author's Note

This book is based on my actual experiences and reflects my perception of the past, present and future. The personalities, events, actions and conversations portrayed within the story have been reconstructed from my memory and the memories of participants. In an effort to safeguard individual privacy, I have changed the names of certain people and, in some cases, altered otherwise identifying characteristics. Events involving the characters happened as described; only minor details have been changed.

Table of Contents

x   Contents

Acknowledgements

I wish to thank Barbara Richardson and Lisa Leitz, sisters and midwives of this book; my writing professor, John Keeble, who impressed upon me the importance of patience during a writer's first ten years; Katherine and John McAnulty for unconditional love; Amy Lutz Yotopoulos and Jason Yotopoulos for their conviction that the book would happen; Laura Lutz for her wise and courageous spirit; Philip Red Eagle for teaching me about ceremony; Ann and Pete Hilderman for being family; Theresa, Curtis and Ashley Nelson for their constancy; Martin Knutsen for his friendship; Lee Machado for long walks; Bryan Hall for many awakenings of the heart; the Guice and Concannon/Hopkins families, for being great neighbors; Laura Cates and Darlene Cherry for introducing me to shipping; Ursula Canci for her courage; Dana Andrews, Reba Jean Cain and Skye MacGregor for insight; Jo Ogden for reading the first draft; Tom Jenks and David Vann for commenting on early drafts; Sherry Wade, Toni Morgan and Sheryl Guice for proofreading; Robert Hauk for introducing me to Marine Engineer Ed Garrahy, who shared his expertise regarding ships and engines; Merchant Marine Engineer Joe Erskine, who taught me about engine room boilers; Lieutenant JG

Jeffrey Piles, Yeoman Second Class Sean Morton, and Lieutenant Commander Karen Phillips, Coast Guard, for sharing their storm stories; John McCurdy, Seattle Branch Agent at Marine Engineers Beneficial Association, for sharing his storm story; my agent, Jodie Rhodes, for continued faith and support; my editors, Lynda Hatch and Joan Dunphy, for their professional assistance; my production manager, Rebecca Sheil, my ballast in the editorial process. To those whose contributions I have inadvertently neglected to mention, please accept my apologies. I am grateful to all.

It should also be noted that although I have used my name, the name of the ship and the names of other people within these pages are purely fictional.

Prologue

My dear daughters Lisa and Emily,

Remember when I told you about my childhood dream of sailing the high seas in search of adventure? Well, I hope both of you are sitting down right now, because I've decided to rekindle that lost desire and ship out with the merchant marines. It all started a few months ago when my friend at the YMCA, Cheryl, told me that women could work in the shipping industry. I haven't been able to get my thoughts of sailing the high seas out of my mind since then. Just imagine: a college English professor turned seaman. Sounds crazy, I know, but I've decided that this is what I want to do. The only people that I've talked about this with are my friends, Paul and Elizabeth, but now I feel that it is time to tell the two of you. I haven't worked out all the details yet, but I'm planning to give my notice to the English Department this week. I don't know how my colleagues will react to my decision, but I'll tell you more the next time we talk on the phone. Don't worry, I've talked to several people who do this for a living, and they all say it is very safe.

I bet you both are wondering right now, exactly what are the merchant marines? Believe me, I didn't know either. But I have since learned that contrary to what many people think, they are not part of the United States Marines. No, they simply are to the ocean what trucks are to land. The merchant marines are seamen who move cargo from one port to another. In addition to transporting commercial cargo, some of them also have interactions with the government. In Tacoma, they have two ready-reserved ships, manned by merchant marine labor, whose specific purpose is to be ready to assist in times of war. Loaded with supplies, they can sail off to wherever they are needed at any given moment. The two sitting in Tacoma port are The Cape Island and The Cape Intrepid. It's very unlikely that I will be assigned to one of those. I've heard that most first timers get assigned to a commercial ship like a tanker or grain freighter.

I'm sure you two are still in shock reading this letter. Trust me, you are not alone. Even though it was my dream, never did I imagine the possibility that such an adventure would really come true.

I promise to write often to you both with the latest on my seafaring exploits.

All My Love,

Mom

Chapter One

If Only

I lie awake as a warm breeze sweeps through my open bedroom window. The night air carries with it the sounds of a city still stirring. I listen to the boats entering Hale Passage, the shouts and laughter of young revelers on the beach and the shriek of a car's squealing brakes from the street below, all the while, thinking.

I know I've never wanted to leave a place as much as I want to leave Tacoma. Although it has little to do with the city itself. I love my friends, teaching, the mountains, the eagles swooping down off the bluffs, Puget Sound and the smell of Douglas fir. Wanting to leave has nothing to do with this place and everything to do with me and the dead end my life has become.

When I think of saying good-bye to maple leaves—yellowed, flattened on the back road where I walk—or try to picture late afternoons in a different place, one without red and green yard lights that flicker from Fox Island across the water to my midnight windows, I feel a deep sadness. After all, I'll be leaving my home. Every time I cross the Narrows Bridge from downtown Tacoma to the more rural peninsula where I reside, I truly experience a feeling of freedom. I love driving past the open field by the small airport, turning the corner toward the stallion standing in the pasture. Whenever I drive up my street, I get a glimpse of the water between the neighbor's property and my yard. Best of all is the smell of salt water carried by the gusts of southerly winds. No matter how much I love my home, I still feel that I have to move on with my life. I slowly drift off, but it is a restless sleep, and I toss and turn churning my decision over and over in my mind.

I arise the next morning and before I even have time to start the coffee, my best friend Elizabeth's husband, Paul, knocks on my door. He stands there as her emissary. Elizabeth and I have talked endlessly about my idea of working for the merchant marines. She understands how desperately I want to follow my dream as well as my need to make more money, how devastated I am over the breakup with my husband; and why I'm hesitating. Nevertheless, it makes her nervous. She's concerned that I will relocate to Portland and even more apprehensive about my shipping out to sea for long periods of time.

Paul leans on the door frame, his giant body uncurled from his ride over in his beat-up green Honda. His straight black hair hangs down over one eyebrow.

"Hey," he says and hands me a cup of coffee he picked up at the corner store. We slurp in silence. As usual, the coffee tastes like lake water. "Did you make your decision?"

"Yeah. I'm going to Portland and entering the merchant marines."

He looks at me from above the rim of his coffee cup. "You sure that is what you want to do?"

I just smile and add more cream to my coffee. A moment later I reply, "I know one thing for sure. My life here is a mess."

"You're being too hard on yourself. We've all made bad choices somewhere along the way," he says.

"Yeah, but there comes a time to get them right."

Paul walks out the back door and onto my rooftop deck, which overlooks Fox Island. The morning sun skitters through the trees to the east. I walk to the doorway and stand a few feet behind him, gazing down at the harbor where a red boat bobs beside the dock. I stare at the serene water.

"I have to tell you. Elizabeth and I think this is the craziest damn thing you've ever thought of doing," he says over his shoulder.

"And I think it's the sanest. No matter what anyone thinks, I need to do this."

I walk back inside and start sorting my clothes into "keep" or "give-away" piles. Throwing two pair of tight Levis on top of the give-away pile, I think about the unique friendship I have with Paul and Elizabeth. A few years after we became friends, it suddenly dawned on me that even during those times I hadn't called them for help, one or both of them mysteriously showed up on my doorstep whenever I needed someone. We have a sixth sense about each other.

I find Paul outside feeding the sunflower seeds to the squirrels who visit everyday. He knows their names are Peter, Paul and Mary, but he still calls them all Paul. I can sense he is aware of my presence but he doesn't attempt to argue his case any further just then.

"I just need to do this." I slump my shoulders and sigh.

He turns around to face me. "It's hard to understand why a highly educated woman like yourself would suddenly and for no apparent reason, drop everything she has worked so hard to accomplish because she has a strong urge to leave everyone and everything she knows to work at sea for the merchant marines."

I frown. "That's not true. You know the reasons."

He looks me square in the face. "You're running away from life instead of hitting it head on."

I hesitate in answering. *Am I running?* I wonder. Is this the same as the time when I was seventeen and I ran away from my father's abuse and my mother's neglect to live with my older sister? My attention is caught by a fat crow on the phone wire who makes strange galump sounds.

Paul steps off the wooden deck onto the tar paper roof. He grabs my fishing pole, which I had left standing in the corner of the porch and begins practicing his casting techniques.

I watch for a few minutes, then I walk to where he stands, sweat dripping from his forehead.

"Sometimes you have to fight," he says.

"I'm not sure that you always have to fight in order to reach the place you belong," I argue. "Sometimes you have to see where life calls you and if that is a long submerged desire, then maybe that is the right place."

He nods and continues to swing the pole up in a circular arc. The slicing sound of the line as it cuts the air and snaps fills my ears. I take a seat on the steps and stare at the morning sky; wisps of white clouds on a blue canvas look more like a painting than the real thing. When I awaken from the trance I notice the sack of sunflower seeds I won't have time to use, seeds I'll leave behind with my dear friends who won't stop trying to take care of me.

Paul leaves when he grows tired of practicing with the fishing pole and has nothing more to say. I remain on the deck, look out at the boats in the harbor and ask the water and sky if I'm doing the right thing. My answer comes later that night in the form of a dream.

A beautiful, translucent woman stands before me, beckoning me to follow. She looks like a life-size Tinkerbell, flitting from one place to another with the flick of a wing. She says her name is Destiny and she seems to be leading me somewhere until she instantly disappears.

"Wait," I say, but she is already gone.

I am in a strange new place where I walk down a dirty green hallway toward a guy sitting behind a desk.

"You gotta get two tattoos if you want to live here. One of the merchant marine emblem and one of a rose," he says.

I think about how I should get the tattoos some-where on my body that won't show, like maybe my butt cheeks.

"Hand's the best place. Just give me your hands and we'll do this real quick like," he says.

It isn't until after I have a tattoo on each hand that it hits me. These marks will be on my hands forever.

I awake in the morning and know exactly what I have to do. I look up the phone number of the Seafarers International Union, dial it and speak with the man in charge, Fred York. In his Boston accent, he says, "Come down to the hall and introduce yourself to the guy with white hair." As soon as I hang up the phone, I grab my purse and keys and leave the house immediately.

Pulling into the Seafarer's International Union parking lot, I check my lipstick in the rearview mirror and remind myself to breathe. I step out of my car and walk toward the front door where groups of guys hang out smoking and talking. I walk casually toward them, my knees barely peeking out of the slit in my long, loose linen skirt that matches the linen vest I wear over a long-sleeved shirt. I look professional, yet feminine.

A man with sandy-colored Ringo-style hair smiles and opens the door for me. I thank him and step into a large open room flanked with windows on the entry side. Pretending to ignore the twenty some pairs of male eyes that gaze my way, I walk straight ahead to the long counter and stand in a short line. A barrel-chested man with white hair leisurely sits on top of a desk doing absolutely nothing while three clerks scramble about helping the men at the front of the line.

"I really like your auburn hair," the white-haired man calls, staring at me. I immediately pick up on his thick Boston accent, the same accent I heard earlier this morning on the phone.

"You must be Fred York," I reply.

His eyes linger on my head. "I really like your auburn hair," he repeats.

I stiffen, my eyes darting about to see if anyone has been listening to this bizarre exchange. I silently pray that Mr. York doesn't make a move on me. Then I go back to worrying about my real reason for being here. This feels more intimidating than anything I have ever done.

"I guess you're the one that I came to see," I say almost timidly.

"First, who are you?" he asks.

"I'm Jeanne," my voice is firmer now.

He smiles, "Okay. You're right, I'm Fred. Come back to my office. Let's talk."

A closed gate separates the waiting room from the hallway that leads to Fred's office. When I try to open it, the latch on the back side won't budge, and since I can't see how it's put together I feel around with my fingers. I begin to panic after searching for a few seconds. I frantically feel around for the opening so that Fred won't have to walk all the way down his side of the railing to open it for me. As Fred watches with what looks to be amusement, I become even more nervous. Finally, my fingers press a lever that moves and the gate opens.

"The first test, right?" I say, looking toward Fred. "The gate, I mean."

He smiles and opens his office door. The guys in the waiting room can still see us through the glass.

"Have a seat and relax. You look nervous."

Me nervous? He has no idea. "Thanks," I say, trying not to fidget.

He sits behind his mahogany desk, hands behind his head. "I've always had a thing for auburn hair."

His reiteration of his earlier remark makes the conversation too personal. I let him dig his way out while I keep my gaze on a photo of an oil tanker on the wall.

"It's unusual," he says, seeming to feel the need to explain his fixation on my hair color. "Guys are intrigued by it."

"Interesting," I say as I silently wonder where this conversation is going.

"So you want to work for the merchant marines." He's leaning forward now, elbows on his desk, hands folded, serious and ready to talk business.

I turn my focus back to Fred, "Yes. I've always dreamed of a life at sea—the excitement, the adventure—and I need to make some money."

"Well, you'll start with at least three thousand a month as a steward assistant. Take home, maybe four. Depends on the ship," he says.

I take a deep breath. "Actually Fred, I want to be a deck hand, an ordinary. I want to learn navigation."

He stifles a smile. "That might be kind of hard at the beginning, especially on the ship I'd like to place you on at the outset. This ship doesn't have many slots for ordinaries."

"If I ship as a steward assistant on my first assignment, will it be possible to switch to deck hand on the next?" I ask.

"I think so. You know, I like intelligent women. You really want to learn navigation?"

I nod. "Very much." I detect the aroma of coffee brewing in the waiting room and take a deep whiff of the strong smell hoping it will help steady my nerves.

"I like women who are smarter than me. Being with an intelligent woman makes me look intelligent."

I try focusing in on his forehead. It's hard to keep a straight face after hearing that line.

"I'm gonna call another office now and find out what you need to get started." He turns his back to pick up the phone receiver from a long narrow table behind his desk. It crashes to the floor.

"Goddamnit."

"Can I help you?" I offer.

"No. I can do it."

He picks up the base of the phone. It's in pretty bad shape, and the more he tries to fix it, the more tangled the line gets. His hands begin to shake.

"I used to work in the engine room. I know how to put things together," he says. He catches me staring at the mess of plastic and wire in his hands.

A young clerk comes into Fred's office to ask a question.

"Damon, this is Jeanne," Fred says. "She wants to sign on with the merchant marines." Damon nods in my direction, but looks distracted. "What can I do for ya?" Fred asks the clerk.

"I need to talk to you privately," Damon answers.

They excuse themselves and speak quietly outside Fred's office door. I get up and walk over to the window where I look out toward the street. I am trying to give them some privacy, but I still hear parts of their whispered conversation.

When Damon leaves, Fred returns to his desk and tells me what I'll need.

"You'll need to get a money order for $220. The physical and drug tests you have to take are in Seattle. Talk to Damon before you leave today and he'll give you the contact information. Get back in touch with me when all that's done."

"Thanks, Fred." I extend my hand, but he waves it away.

"And do me a favor when you talk to Damon," he says before I reach the door. "Ask him his opinion about a woman being a deck hand. I feel strongly we need to ship you as a GSU."

"GSU?" I ask.

"General steward utility. Just another fancy way of saying steward assistant."

I walk out into the waiting room where I see Damon in the corner talking on the telephone. There are information pamphlets strewn across the table, so I leaf through them while I wait for Damon to get off the phone.

Finally he is free. "Hi, I just met you in Fred's office,"
I say.

"Yes, I know. What can I do for you?"

"Could you give me the address and phone number
for the place I need to go to for the physical and drug tests?"

He nods and writes the information down on the
back of an envelope.

"Thanks… Oh and Fred wanted me to ask your opinion about a woman being a deck hand."

"You want my honest opinion?" He looks me over
from head to toe.

I try not to react. "Yes I do."

"I don't think women should be deck hands. I think
they should stay in the steward department. Come here, let
me feel your biceps."

I step back to keep my biceps to myself, but I flex
them so he can see. "Look, I'm strong. I grew up on a farm."

"You could probably do it. But you have to watch
your hands and feet. When a line tightens or snaps, it's easy
to lose a foot or hand."

"Thanks," I say with a smile. "I will."

"Oh, and ah, you know, as men we're used to protect-
ing women, doing things for them, you know? So when you're
tying up or something, a guy might say, 'Here you go honey,'
not meaning it in a bad way but just sort of being helpful."

"I see. So what if a woman came on as a deck hand
and asks questions like, 'Hey, can you show me how to do

that?' And then, after a couple of tries, she gets it right and makes an honest effort to always pull her load."

"Yep. That'd be okay. Just do the job," he repeats. "Just do the job."

In my car I think about how working as a merchant marine seems surprisingly similar to teaching: show up and do your best. Only now I'll make three, maybe four times as much money and my old dream of a thrilling venture on the sea will come true.

From my apartment I call my daughters, who by now have received my letter and are aware of my plan to work at sea. I haven't spoken with either of them since I sent the letter, so I'm not sure how they took my news that I've decided to give the merchant marines a try.

I reach my older daughter, Emily, first. "You're sure this is safe?" she asks, obviously still in shock over my decision. "What about all those men aboard the ship? You'll be one of a few women or even the only woman. And what about the storms and war zones?"

I tell her not to worry. "Ten or fifteen years ago it was a different story, but now women are doing things no one ever dreamed we could. Remember what I said to you in my letter—the merchant marines haul commercial cargo from one port to another. They are the truckers of the sea. Even though they sometimes interact with the government, I will make sure that I am assigned to a commercial voyage." Although that calms Emily a bit, I can tell that she doesn't feel very reassured.

My younger daughter Lisa's reaction is exactly the opposite. "I have been excited for you since I read your letter," she says enthusiastically. "Go for it, Mom. Just think of it as exciting, hard-working therapy that you get paid for."

The therapy starts the next morning when I dial the Seattle number to set up an appointment for the seaman's physical. I get an automated message asking me to hold and saying that my call will be taken in the order received. It will be approximately a ten minute wait. I press the speaker button on my phone, hang up the receiver and listen to Muzak. Two pigeons strutting on the roof distract me. My mind revolves backward, and I start questioning my past life. The *what ifs* and *if onlys* swirl in my head.

Married to a military officer, moving every other year, I raised two daughters on the run. I worked on the run too, a series of low-paying odd jobs that traveled well. Office assistant, actress, teaching English to German speaking adults, drama coach and visual artist, just to name a few. Never enough time to establish myself.

My marriage started to fall apart when I attended graduate school and received an M.F.A. in Creative Writing. At the time an M.F.A. seemed logical when I

*thought about making a living in education, but in ret-
rospect, it wasn't logical at all. The only jobs I could find
were teaching adjunct English classes for slave wages at
several community colleges. I found out very soon that
only twenty-five percent of classes are taught by full-
time, salaried professors. The other seventy-five percent
of the college classes are taught by adjunct instructors.
Like everyone else who teaches part-time, however, I
began with the hope that the officials would be so
impressed with my qualifications that I'd be one of the
chosen few to leap from adjunct to assistant professor.*

*I poured my heart and mind into teaching for
$1200 a month without benefits. I wanted the full-time
status, the intellectual freedom and the $40,000 a year
with benefits that full-time professors received. After five
years I realized it wasn't going to happen.*

*After my divorce I crashed on Elizabeth and Paul's
floor. Then I found the studio apartment and later a tiny
bungalow. As I got into the single life I kept thinking if
only I were experienced in dating and knew how to
choose a good man. Of course this didn't happen, as I
made some bad choices.*

*Then there's the legacy of my divided family. My
father still professes his innocence of abusing me and all
my siblings believe him. He wants to clear things up, but
the jagged past won't disappear. It plagues me.*

When my sister called to say Dad was very ill, perhaps even dying, I told her, "I'm leaving my teaching job and am planning to ship out with the merchant marines soon. Please tell Dad I said 'hello' and though I will always love him, I still don't want to see him."

The line went dead.

The Muzak abruptly stops and I am brought back to reality by a woman's voice on the line asking, "How can I help you?"

Chapter Two

Stepping Into Thin Air

Having taken care of the multiple tasks and medical proce-
dures to make my dream a reality, I'm back in Union Hall.
Money order in one hand and the results of my physical and
drug test in the other, I'm going to talk with Fred York about
the next step in my signing on with the merchant marines.
This time I'm more relaxed. Several of the guys who'd been
in the waiting room on my first visit nod, smile and say hello.
They drink coffee, read the local newspapers and gossip
about shipping. Ship gossip is part of getting the jobs. So and
so hears that such and such ship is crewing up in two weeks
and will need an AB (able bodied seaman), a chief cook and
a third engineer. That kind of gossip.

The job calls occur every hour on the hour, but since it's only 9:20 A.M., there are no lines. I walk right up to Damon's desk and tell him I'm back and I've got all the things Fred asked me to get. "Go on back there," he points his thumb to the door behind him, "Fred's been waiting for you."

Sitting behind that giant mahogany desk, Fred looks like an executive, and without so much as a greeting, he jumps right into a lecture.

"If you don't hear but one thing I ever say to you, hear this. The worst thing a woman shipper can do is to sleep with someone on a ship, especially an officer," Fred says with deep sincerity.

"Fred, I can assure you that I have never slept with a coworker and have no intention of doing so in the future. By the way," I motion my hand to the chair next to me, "do you mind if I sit down?"

He sheepishly smiles, embarrassed for his lack of manners and nods toward the empty chair. Before I've even landed in the seat, he's returned to his speech. "You know, there's engineers and guys like that out there. They tell you they're not married when they really are. Hell, they've got wives and kids at home. But they're out at sea, they're a long way from home and they're lonely."

He stops, raises both arms, his hands point away from his head as if asking a question. I don't say a word. I figure he's on a roll and to interrupt would be to miss the salient points of his story and his philosophy of proper employee behavior. Dramatically, he lowers his arms onto his desk.

"You're a smart woman and you might meet a smart guy, fall in love and end up sleeping together. Everyone will find out, no matter how secretive you try to be. Then, the first time you accidentally ignore another guy or mess up in some way, they all will look down their noses at you and say, 'That fucking whore!'"

I'm shocked. "Really?"

"You betcha. You betcha, kiddo."

"Wow." I didn't know if I really wanted to hear this speech when Fred first started, but now I'm feeling grateful for his wisdom and advice.

"You gotta remember that working out there on the sea isn't the same as a regular job where you go home at night. At sea, when you go home, it's up a flight or two of stairs. Your room might be next to the guy's or one floor above or below. You start messing around and within one day, one day I'm telling you, the whole ship knows."

"I see." I look down at my folded hands in my lap.

"I hope you really do see," he says, obviously relishing the role of over-protective patriarch, "because you got thirty guys out there and if one guy scores, you now got twenty-nine guys who resent the hell outta you and are just waiting for you to make some kind of a mistake so they can let you know how pissed off they are."

By the time he finishes, I'm speechless. He stares at me, waiting for a response. I'm wondering about the reason behind this sex talk. I know merchant marine ships had numerous sexual harassment law suits ten years back. Maybe now they're being hypervigilant about gender issues.

I look up at him again, "Fred, as I said before, I have no intention of getting involved with a coworker."

"Good girl. Believe me. Make your life easier out there and treat every guy the exact same way. Don't give anyone any more attention than anyone else. Got it?"

"I got it, Fred."

"I can't tell you how many women have sat in that chair you're sitting in and cried their hearts out because they didn't listen to me."

"Fred, I got it."

"Good. And one more thing. I'm shipping you as a steward assistant. If you do okay this time out and still want to try the deck department, we'll do that the second time around."

"No chance of changing your mind for this trip?"

"None," he states firmly. "Now get over to the coast guard and get your Z card so we can get you on a ship."

"Z card?" I ask.

"Seaman's ID card, pretty much like a driver's license. If you want to drive, you have to have a driver's license. If you want to be in the merchant marines, you have to have a Z card."

Suddenly, I feel like I'm in someone else's movie.

It is one of the hottest days of the summer and I'm driving to Coast Guard Pier 36 in Seattle to get my Z card. I have everything I need in order to obtain it: passport, birth certificate, social security card, record of coast guard physical exam, negative TB test and proof of payment. Two guys in the waiting room are having a technical merchant marine talk and, even though I only understand every other word they say, I try not to let it unnerve me.

After a few minutes the steel-gray haired woman at the counter calls my name and hands me a clipboard. "Fill these forms out, three pages front and back. Bring it back when you're done."

It's easy to notice other, more interesting things when you're filling out boring repetitive forms. I look more closely at the guy sitting to my right wearing khaki shorts, carrying a brown brief case, eating a chocolate bar and a banana. Food-wise, my kind of guy. Nearby are two older men who are talking about the ships they've been on. I lean forward in my chair to listen in the hope of learning some of this new language. I study the bearded man in his mid-forties whose pre-school son keeps asking him why they have to stay in Seattle for so long. The boy can't keep his eyes off the thin man at the counter whose feet shuffle like a tap dancer.

I finally finish filling out my forms and turn them in. A few minutes later, a muscle-bound man calls me over for finger printing.

He demonstrates how to roll the top of a finger back and forth several times on the ink, then carefully roll it just one time on the paper, slowly right to left, then lift off. Now it's my turn to do the rest. After I do each individual finger pad and both thumbs twice, the man tells me to do all four fingers together in one row, also twice.

"We give these to the FBI," he says.

I snap my head up and look wide-eyed at him.

He studies at my face. "You'd be surprised at how many people leave the country illegally through the merchant marines."

"Escaping a terrible past?" I ask.

He nods. "All you have to do now is take the oath and have your picture taken. Wait here."

I lean up against the wall and wait for my name to be called. The big hand on the clock ticks methodically, marking the seconds I spend standing there. The numbers on its face begin to blur as my mind wanders.

"Escaping a terrible past." The words fit my situation perfectly. I'm middle aged and still trying to figure it all

out. Dad's in his seventies. The cards I sent him the past few years on his birthdays and for Father's Day were probably a good thing, but I haven't seen him in years. That's a long time not to talk. Maybe wanting him to acknowledge the truth is asking too much. Maybe I should have pretended none of it ever happened, but I couldn't then or now...

Dad must remember what he did all those nights when Mom worked late. He must remember waking me out of sleep and carrying me to the downstairs bedroom. When I became an adult with my own children, I called to tell him I remembered all of it, remembered stopping him when I was six, remembered later kicking the shit out of him one morning while Mom slept in.

When I made that call he threatened me in the same menacing tone he used when I was little. "Why you little shit. You better be glad I'm not there 'cause if I were, I'd knock some sense into you."

Again, he tried to silence me.

"And would you tell people I was crazy too?" I asked. "And would men in white coats come to take me away if I ever dared tell anyone what you did to me?"

"Why you little heifer. I'll get you."

His threat didn't scare me as it had when I was a small child, but it still rattled me to the core. Since that phone call, I haven't talked to him, only written. After that day, talking with him or seeing him again has just been too frightening. I told the truth and although men in white coats didn't come to take me away, I lost the rest of my family. I lost them to their denial and to their silence.

I wipe away a tear from the corner of my eye as I wait for the coast guard officer to call me for my Z card photo. I'm still preoccupied with thoughts of my father, but I am trying to clear my mind. Somehow I start thinking about the ocean and how I will be sailing the high seas very soon as a member of the merchant marines. I have come this far in my life and am going to live my dream shortly. My spirits start to rise. I feel my worries slip away, excitement and anticipation filling me.

As I begin to smile again, I hear my name being called. "Okay, James and Jeanne," the coast guard official says, "I'll swear you both in at the same time."

James, whom I've never seen before today, and I walk over to where the official is standing.

"Just answer 'I will or I do.' Do you swear to uphold the coast guard, etc."

"I will," I say.

I look at James, a tall, hairy beast of a man, and say, "Does this mean we're married?" He slants his gray eyes over at me and doesn't laugh. Neither does the heavyset woman or the big man who shuffles the paperwork. In fact, all three of them frown at me.

The woman looks over and exchanges glances with the man doing paperwork. He then scribbles something on one of the forms and says, "Okay, come on. Let's get your pictures taken."

As I face the camera I cannot decide whether I am supposed to smile or not. If I smile, will they think I won't take my job seriously? If I don't, will they think I am having second thoughts about this decision? Before I even make up my mind, a bright white light flashes in my face, blinding me for a moment. "Next," the woman says. So much for simple decisions.

I take a look at my Z card as soon as it is available. The photo didn't come out too well. I'm smiling but not as big as I usually do. I suspect it was because of the reaction to my joke, but I cast my cares away about how I look. Who looks at the card anyway? I am going to be a seaman. I am going to live my dream.

But I begin to question my motives again as I walk out to the parking lot. *Am I really doing the right thing?* So many changes. Maybe fulfilling my dream of going to sea is too much? I shake my head to get rid of any negative thoughts. Never. All I have to do now is hang out in the union hall until I get a ship. The finality of it feels over-whelming, but I am ready.

I find my car sitting in the bright sunlight. When I unlock the door, the wave of heat that hits me lets me know that it is scorching hot inside. I slowly climb in and place one hand on the steering wheel, then snatch it away. It's too hot to touch. I shift in my seat trying to get comfortable against the sticky, hot vinyl. I put the keys in the ignition, roll down the windows and sit in the sweltering heat while I wait for the car to cool. After a few moments, the air conditioning kicks in. I pull the car out of the parking spot to wait at the lot's entrance for a break in a long line of big trucks.

I'm back in the union hall. I've jumped through the hoops, paid my bills for the next three months, moved from Tacoma to Portland, and now I'm waiting for a ship assignment. I chat with Tim, Pat and Bart, three guys who have been camped out here longer than I have. I listen to the ship gossip that could get me an assignment.

Bart says, "The worst ship anyone can get assigned to is a grain ship. You seldom, if ever, have shore leave."

"You stay on the tub for close to forever," Tim adds. "When a grain ship reaches its destination, it usually is a far away place that's dirty and disgusting."

Bart continues, "Locals come on board to unload the grain. It's often as low-tech as going in the hole, filling bags and manually hauling out the cargo. The ship often stays there for a month or more, waiting for the cargo to be unloaded. It's usually in trouble spots too, like Afghanistan, Saudi Arabia and Indonesia. All you'd see of the world is your crew mates."

"And the best ship I could get?" I ask.

"You won't get a good one as a C-Book," Pat says.

I look at him with uncertainty. "C-Book?"

"There are three departments, Steward, Deck and Engine, and within each of those departments, the personnel moves up from C-Book, to B-Book and finally, to A-Book. When a job position comes up on the job board, A and B Books beat out C-Books within each department."

I come in everyday of the week and listen to the gossip. I do my best to learn the terminology and to be patient as I wait to get an assignment.

Week two seems to be bringing me more of the same. I'm back in the union hall waiting room hoping for an assignment when, to my surprise, in walks another woman. In a thick southern accent, she introduces herself as Ruby Marie. "But you can call me Ruby." Now I'm not the only female waiting for a ship. Long, blond hair frames her ruddy complexion and her incredible turquoise eyes. Within ten minutes she gives me the short version of her life story. "I've been married and divorced twice. I have five kids, the youngest is fourteen and lives with his father," she rattles on without pausing for a breath. "I can't pay all my bills. My new boyfriend is an engineer for the merchant marines. It was his idea for me to join. He figures once in a while we'll get on the same ship, but I hope we don't on my first time out. I want to do my first run solo. I want to feel independent."

She casually asks for my story. Up until now I've felt safe around all the guys. Men don't usually ask those kinds of questions. I quickly run through a couple scenarios in my mind and come up with an abbreviated version.

"I was an adjunct instructor at a college with no hope of a full-time job," I say.

"So honey, you're going from teaching to toilets?"

I feel my face redden and decide to change the subject. "You know, I have a friend who says she feels like she was sleep-walking the first forty years of her life, that she wasn't fully awake until after her alcoholic husband died." I hope someone else's story will satisfy her curiosity.

Lush black lashes dance around Ruby's eyes when she asks, "But what woke you up?"

Silence fills the air. "This is difficult," I say as I stop to think. "Three things, I guess." I feel exposed. I wish I could be more like Ruby and open my heart to a stranger. My stomach feels like it's in a blender. I don't know if it's the questions, the men sitting within earshot or the fact that I've been here almost two weeks waiting eight hours a day for a job. Tears stick in my throat.

Ruby is either more sensitive than she appears to be or I'm more transparent than I'd like to think I am. "Come on, girl," she nudges my arm, "let's take a walk. We've got thirty minutes before the next call."

We walk a few blocks to a nearby cafe and sit in the open air drinking coffee. Ruby waits in silence, looking at me now and then to see how I'm coping.

I feel like I'm meeting with a therapist. "I woke up a few weeks ago on my birthday," I begin, "and admitted I was a divorcee working in a dead-end job that didn't pay the bills and would never offer any advancement, benefits or retirement, and all the dreams that I once had of adventure were beginning to dry up. Then I heard that my estranged father only has a few months to live. My family refuses to believe the abuse I suffered at his hands when I was a child. It kills me to know that they believe I imagined it." I pause and look at an empty table nearby, wishing for a moment that I could sit there and become someone else. Reluctantly, I return to my life and focus again on my conversation with Ruby. She hasn't moved.

"Nothing was working, so I figured it was time to do the thing I always wanted to do: take a new tack and have a daring and thrilling experience."

Ruby looks at me, her heart soaking up my story. She reaches over and pats my hand. "Oh honey. You're a strong woman. I've got a good feeling about you, a real good feeling."

Week three in the union hall and still no GSU jobs. I walk up
to Fred York. "Aren't you tired of looking at my face?"

"As a matter of fact, I am tired of looking at your
unhappy mug. Okay, regardless what ship comes up on the
board next, you have to take it."

"I will, I will," I promise.

He shakes his head, "Be here for the one o'clock call."

I have some time for lunch, so I drive out to the fish
market on the waterfront and buy crab spread and crackers.
I sit at a picnic table where I can watch the boat traffic in the
harbor. When a large container ship enters the harbor, I picture myself working on it: a tiny little ant next to those towering multicolored containers. Scared and excited, I worry
that I might miss something at the hall. I'm still hungry but
I stop eating and drive back for the one o'clock call.

The place is buzzing. More people than usual are
here sitting around waiting for jobs. Ruby is here waiting
with them. Fred walks up to the big white board behind the
counter, calls out the jobs and slips the cards into their slots.
"One AB Watch Stander on the Overseas Illinois. One GSU
on the O.S. Illinois."

The guy to my left elbows me and says, "Get the hell
up there." An excited Ruby jumps up and down.

Orange card in hand, I dash toward the counter, but
a new guy wearing a white Nehru shirt throws in his B-Card.
No one has seen this mystery man before. Fred apologizes,
"I'm sorry, but he beat you out."

I tap my card on the counter. Where did this guy come from? I have been waiting here for over two weeks. I deserve this job. *Only in my universe would this happen*, I think. I decide to take a break and turn around to walk outside when Fred barks my name. "Hey Jeanne. Stick around. This guy doesn't have his drug test."

I wait until the two o'clock call. Nothing. Three o'clock. Fred calls about the drug test. No word. The waiting is killing me. Do I really have a chance of getting this job or not?

After four hours of waiting, Fred turns to the white shirt guy, "If your drug test isn't in by the nine o'clock call tomorrow morning, I'm giving the job to her." He points to me. My spirits rise a little, but once again I don't want to get my hopes up too high with the way my luck has been going.

I go home and try to get some rest, but it's no use. I'm so pumped with adrenaline I could run twenty miles straight. I really want this job badly. Correction: I need this job. Tossing and turning in bed, the hours leisurely roll by. How can you sleep when you have been working so hard for a job and a dream and you are this close? All I can do is lie here watching the hours tick by on the bedroom clock.

The alarm clock never gets a chance to sound this morning. I get up, take a shower and drive down to the union hall as fast as I can. I want to know what my fate is, but there is nothing on the board at nine o'clock. The guy with the B-Card is back, but this time his shirt is blue. He stands beside the counter with a forlorn look on his face talking with Fred while I fidget in my seat and wait.

A guy sitting nearby makes me even more nervous. He sighs, opens his eyes wide, makes big gestures with his arms and talks too loud. I try to play it cool and get a package of peanut M&Ms from the vending machine. I leave the blue ones in the bag and eat all the rest. People aren't meant to eat the color blue, I tell myself.

Ten o'clock. No jobs. Same at eleven. All this time, the guy with the blue shirt hangs around the counter talking with Fred, who stares into the computer screen, waiting for some kind of cyber vision.

Finally, Fred looks at blue shirt. "Okay amigo, I've given you plenty of extra hours and it's still a no go. I've got to fill this job. I'm shipping her." He points to me.

Defeated, the man in the blue shirt walks away, looking stunned. I feel slightly akin to a vulture, but I can live with it knowing how badly I need and want this job.

I hand Fred my Z card, my orange card, my shot records and passport. He sifts through them, and asks, "Where's your benzene card?" He's talking loud enough to be heard in the next state.

"The doctor wouldn't give me a benzene test, because I've never shipped before."

Now he's yelling, screaming that he told me to have a passport, a drug test and a benzene test. He's leaning across the counter into my face, his eyebrows one inch away from mine. "I told you that if you got an oil tanker, you'd need a benzene test. And this assignment, little lady, is an oil tanker."

He dials someone on the phone and barks to the receiving end, "Hey. I got an entry GSU with no benzene card. Can I ship her on a tanker? Well what do you know. Yeah, you're a piece of shit too. It's a tanker. Ship her?"

He hangs up the phone. His face is splotchy as if he got pelted with a tomato. The veins pop out on his forehead. "We're shipping you. Oil tanker to Alaska. You're going to work your ass off."

"Thank you, thank you," I say, completely relieved and full of smiles.

Tonight, I can barely keep my eyes closed for five minutes, my excitement getting the better of me. I remember being this way growing up. Whenever I wanted something, whether it was a new bicycle or going somewhere special with a friend, all my pent up energy would build until I got what I wanted. *I haven't wanted anything this badly in a long while*, I think. I stare up at the ceiling of my room and watch the shadows from the fir tree outside dance around. It's too good to be true. I keep going over my assignment in my mind reassuring myself. I'll be on a tanker that picks up oil in Alaska, delivers it to California or Washington, then runs back up the coast for more oil. I'll finally be a member of the merchant marines. With that thought in my head I fall asleep.

I dream about Lynn Perry, the teenage lifeguard who taught me how to jump off the high dive the summer I turned seven. All of us young girls had hero worshipped Lynn; she was the teenage girl we hoped to be one day. I trained for that moment all summer, going from one swimming lesson to another, learning how to float, to side stroke, to do the crawl, all the way to swimming to the deep end, reserved for the "real" swimmers.

Then Lynn convinced me that using the low board was no different than jumping off the side of the pool, so I tried it. She was right, except for that extra little bit of spring the board had. After that, I jumped off the low board every afternoon for a week. I'm not sure what made Lynn think I was ready for the high dive, but she started talking to me about it, how diving from that height was so much fun, how she knew I could do it. Convincing as she was, I shook my head no until she said something that made me reconsider. She said, "If you try it just once, I'll be down in the water waiting for you. Nothing bad can possibly happen to you because I'll be right there."

So I did just what she told me to do. I stood in line for the high dive with all the big kids. We all were shivering as water dripped off our bodies in the shade of the big oaks that lined the fence behind the pool. Then I climbed the ladder one foot at a time, just like she said and the big boys didn't even give me a hard time about it. In fact, they encouraged me. When I got to the top, I followed Lynn's directions exactly. I listened for her voice from the water saying she was there waiting for me; then I began walking forward on the diving board, not looking down or stopping. I kept walking until my last step was into air.

Moments later I found myself in the water and Lynn was right there beside me.

When I wake from my dream, I'm still thinking of Lynn and the lesson she taught me that summer. I resolve to conquer my new challenge—going to sea—as I did the high dive as a child: One step at a time.

Chapter Three

Erratic Heart Beat

Only a few days later I board the late afternoon flight on the small eight person commuter plane from SeaTac to Port Angeles, Washington. During the flight the plane hits some bad turbulence and the bumpy ride shakes up most of the passengers, but it doesn't faze me in the least. I'm already catatonic. As we circle the airport in preparation for landing, I get a glimpse of the small airstrip, which is bordered on one side by the Olympic Mountains and the other by the Strait of Juan de Fuca.

There are two big ships in the harbor. One boasts a tall blue stack, a green flat deck and a rectangular white house. It looks astonishingly large and foreboding. I begin to wonder about the crew that works on a ship that massive. What kind of people are chipping paint on the upper deck, chopping vegetables in the galley, polishing brass on the bridge, tightening bolts in the engine room? My palms start to sweat. Intuitively, I know this is my ship. I can feel the muscles in my neck and back tense as I start to worry about the conditions I will be facing. What will my room look like? How big will it be? Will I have to share a bathroom or will I have my own? What was I thinking when I committed to this job? Am I really up for this?

The plane lands smoothly and I have no problem gathering my bags and calling a taxi. As we load my three duffel bags into the trunk, I ask the driver, "When we're dockside, could you help carry my bags onto the ship?"

"I'll take them outta the taxi, but no way up the gangplank. No gangplank." He looks at me as if I'm an alien.

Great. Just Great. Then I remember how things usually work out for me. On the thirty-minute ride, I talk about the weather, about Port Angeles and about the ship I will soon be boarding. He confirms my belief that the O.S. Illinois is the big one with the blue stack sitting in the port. After our conversation and a brief silence, he undergoes a change of heart.

"I'll see what the situation looks like when we get there and help as much as I can." He looks back at me in the rearview mirror, eyes recanting.

I smile back at him. "Thanks a lot."

He's now watching the road, so he doesn't see my smile nor does he see me raise my arms in victory.

It's way past dinner when we pull into the empty shipyard. The Overseas Illinois looms several stories above us as we drive under her thick, heavy lines tied to the dock. The ship appears even bigger and more intimidating close up than from the air. The tanker appears too large and dense to float or rise up out of the water like a phoenix from the ashes. As I look at her huge, reddish-black hull from the back seat of the cab, I'm shaking so much from anticipation that I can barely open the door. Suddenly, I feel too small for the task. What lured me to this? Dwarfed by this massive hulk of steel, I feel like an ant, yet I realize I am eager to board the vessel and live my new life.

I step out of the taxi and begin discussing my fare with the driver when a tall, greasy-looking guy saunters down the steep plank and hollers, "Are you my replacement?"

"I don't know. My mental telepathy is disengaged at the moment so I don't know who you are," I say, joking because I'm nervous.

"Marty," he says, extending his hand. "The steward assistant." It's one of very few things he says within the next hour that I am able to understand.

I shake his hand. "Jeanne," I reply. "Your replacement."

Marty picks up one of my smaller bags. He cusses as he carries it the entire fifty feet up the gang plank. The cabby carries the other mini-bag. I haul the biggest, heaviest duffel. The moose.

"If you think that one's heavy, you should try this one," I tell the cabby, who doesn't laugh until I slip him a twenty at the top. Then he smiles, his smoked-stained teeth glistening in the evening twilight. The fare is seven bucks.

On the peeling, rusted green deck I walk behind Mr. Mumbles toward the house, the big white building on the stern. Despite the rattling sound which makes me fear for my life, a tiny elevator whisks us to B Deck where Marty shows me his old room—my new room. Smelling of strawberry air freshener and mildew, the grimy walls halt any fantasies I've entertained about having a cozy, comfortable nook. With his two suitcases and my three duffel bags in the room, we're almost shoulder-to-shoulder.

"Are you single?" he asks.

It's the second thing he says that I can understand. "Yeah," I say. "Who wants to know?"

He winks. I already know this guy is not my cup of tea. Although he is lean and not bad looking, he just does not fit my mold of a man. The slicked back, greasy hair and overly macho bravado just does not do it for me.

"I've had many single women," he brags. "Would you like to go ashore with me?"

"No," I say bluntly.

His leering smile fades quickly before he turns on his heel, walks out the door and mutters something about showing me the ship. I can't believe my first day on board is beginning like this. Marty turns back and motions to me to follow him.

We climb a flight of stairs to C Deck, where Marty points to a broom closet, mutters something about engineers, then leads me up another flight of stairs to D Deck. Here we walk past five rooms arranged in a square hallway. For the entire tour I am practically running in order to keep up with Marty. It is very tough to keep up with him and his short, but quick steps. He is obviously in a hurry. The tour is even more confusing because D and C Decks have almost identical floor plans with five mates on D and five engineers on C. The most I can decipher from Marty's incoherent ramblings and hands waving about is that the second mate gets up early. His room must be cleaned early. Others can wait.

Back on the stairwell we come upon a wiry, but well-built man standing with his hands on his hips. Wearing faded jeans and a plaid flannel shirt, he appears to be overworked and exhausted. He smells like a Montecristo cigar and stands about six feet tall with a thin mustache and pouty expression. He's handsome with dark hair and wisps of silver around his temples, giving his overall appearance a distinguished yet rugged look.

"Hi," I say casually, nodding my head.

"The captain," Marty points.

Nice introduction, Jeanne.

"I'm Jeanne, the new, uh—the new S.A." I smile awkwardly after fumbling over my new job title. As a former
English professor, "S.A." reminds me of the countless *essays* I
used to grade every week. The more I look at the captain the
more he looks like a benevolent dictator, which doesn't seem
to calm my nerves.

"I'll sign you up tomorrow, probably in the afternoon," the captain says with a strong accent, then walks past
us up the stairs. I can tell he is from the east coast, possibly
from New York.

Back on B Deck, Marty finally picks up his suitcases,
but only after prodding me one last time.

"Are you sure you don't want to go ashore with me?
We could party down."

"I'm so sure you could put money on it," I say.

He turns with a shrug and walks down the drab
green hallway.

I have a private room and bath on B Deck. Mine's the last
room on port side, left back, third floor. I breathe deeply
while taking it all in: the avocado walls, the duct tape patches
barely covering peep-holes which look as if they've been
made by a heavy-duty drill and the filth everywhere. I sit on
the bed because I don't want to sit on the dirty, overstuffed,
cracked vinyl chair that matches my avocado walls and looks
like it hasn't been dusted in the last century. When I walk

into the shower I see so many species of living organisms that describing it would require the use of scientific terms I don't even know.

Everything in this room is some putrid shade of green, including my heart. My heart is the greenest of all. Sitting on this ship about to set sail on a seemingly endless sea is like being in a foreign country. I don't know the language or the customs of my new surroundings. How will I learn what I need to learn? Who will teach me?

I don't know how to relax and stop worrying about everything that I have to figure out. Cleaning always seemed to ease my mind at home, so I look around the room for any cleaning solutions. Peering underneath the sink in the bathroom, I come across a spray bottle of disinfectant and a roll of paper towels. I get up, grab the disinfectant and the paper towels, and start wiping down the entire room. My work slowly helps the look of the room but does little for my nerves. If this is how Marty kept his room, what will the rest of the rooms look like? As I continue cleaning, I cannot help but ask myself if I made the right decision taking this job. I begin making a mental list of the pros and cons of the situation, trying hard to find more pros than cons. Finally, I remind myself that this job is giving me the opportunity to live out my dream—even if it means scrubbing a few foul rooms.

It takes me over three hours to wipe down every area in my new home that Marty may have conceivably touched. I have now unpacked, cleaned and spread my pretty floral throw over the vinyl chair. This room is beginning to look and feel a little more like home. Afraid that I might find out negative information about this oil tanker and jump ship before we set sail in the morning, I decide to stay in my room for the rest of the evening. Stories that I might hear from the crew might be too much for me to handle right now. The problem is, I'm famished from missing both lunch and dinner. Then I remember the small silver box of chocolates Paul and Elizabeth gave to me for emergencies. I reach over and pick it up off the desk. I take off the thin red ribbon and remove the cover to reveal an assortment of sweet delicacies. I eat two small truffles and wash them down with an elixir of protein powder mixed with water in an empty vitamin bottle.

I grab my journal and sit on my bed with the chocolates. Resting here in chocolate euphoria, I start to wonder why the hell I'm the only woman on an oil tanker with a crew of thirty men. I feel like I am basically a well-paid maid. Maybe Paul was right. Maybe I am running away. Maybe I should have stayed and butted heads with the college. Maybe I should have met with my father. Maybe I should stop avoiding things that scare me. But isn't that what joining the merchant marines is all about—taking a bold and adventuresome new path and overcoming my fears?

As I sit up and search for a fresh page in my journal, a few photos I had tucked inside fall to the floor. One is a picture of my daughters and the other is of Elizabeth and

Paul. I pick up the photos and think back to the encouraging words they all spoke during our final conversations before I left for the airport. Now I know that I will be okay. It's like they are all here with me giving me their strength and their love. "Be strong. You can do this," I tell myself. I suddenly realize I have been thinking of quitting before I even started. I have not even given this job and my aspirations a chance before those old self-doubts set in. My spirits rise higher.

As I savor the last piece of chocolate, I hear voices coming from the passageway outside my door. It's probably my boss, the chief steward, who Marty muttered something about arriving late tonight. Although the steward's room is across from mine, I'm not going out there to introduce myself. I'm staying put and meeting him in the galley at five tomorrow morning exactly like the union hall guys told me.

I decide to write a letter to Elizabeth and Paul to pass the time before I go to sleep.

Port Angeles, Washington

Dear Friends,
I've made it to Port Angeles and onto my ship, the Overseas Illinois. She's a huge, old tanker and rumor has it that she's ready to retire but for now, they whisk her in and out of dry dock to the tune of millions of dollars. She's a sight, that's for sure. You

know how military ships look perfect with their gray decks all pristine and shiny? Well, strike that image. This upper deck is a patchwork of mottled green mixed with rust.

I'm lying here on my bunk wondering how I should tell you I already ate the entire box of emergency chocolates you gave me. I know you're laughing right now, but honestly, I had to. It was a real emergency. I hadn't eaten all day and was afraid to leave my room for fear of hearing horror stories of life on this ship that might send me running for shore. Anyway, if you've never had chocolates with a protein powder drink, give it a try. Thank you again for the lovely gift.

My trip to the ship went smoothly. The plane ride was relatively uneventful. After we landed the cab driver who drove me to the port did not want to help me carry my bags up the fifty-foot gangplank. Do you remember how heavy the big duffel bag was? Well, I finally convinced the cabbie to help with my bags—gave him a hefty tip too—but he grabbed the light one and was up the ramp before I could count to one.

Guess what? The first guy from the ship that I met already asked me out on a date. Actually, his pick-up line was: "I have had many single women." Yuck! Needless to say, I rejected his invitation to go ashore this evening. I first met him as he came sauntering down the plank to where the cabbie and I were gathering my bags. Turns out, this guy was the previous Steward's Assistant and the person I am here to replace. Not for nothing, but he didn't seem to have the look of someone that would perform cleaning duties. He introduced himself as Marty and proceeded to mumble almost every word that escaped his lips—except his well-crafted pick-up line—as if his mouth was still full of last night's dinner. I knew right away that it was going to be tough to understand him.

After he gave up on hitting on me, Marty gave me a tour of the ship. He went so fast I was practically sprinting through the maze of floors and rooms to keep up with him. The scariest part was the ride on the rickety old elevator. From the sounds that came echoing out of it, I was afraid the elevator was going to fall apart with us in it, but it seemed to do alright. Plus it was a big help in getting my heavy bags up a few flights.

When Marty showed me his old room—my room now—I almost fell over! First of all, it was so small we could barely both fit inside with all our bags lying on the floor. But the size was the least of the room's problems; it was varying shades of putrid green and smelled as bad as it looked. Torn pieces of duct tape barely covered peep-holes in the walls. There must be two dozen of those peep-hole patches. Anyway, the twin bed is wedged end-to-end between the far walls and sits right under a two-by-two foot porthole. A room with a view. Not bad, eh? So, the width of the room equals the length of a twin bed. What is that? About six feet? Not exactly the penthouse at the Ritz.

Oh, and I almost forgot to mention my most embarrassing moment so far. Marty and I passed by this exhausted but handsome man in a stairwell. This guy needed a shave and from the *looks of the bags under his eyes, a good night's sleep. I just said a casual hello as if he were a deck hand or crewmember. It was only then that Marty decided to tell me the man was the ship's captain. Geez! How was I supposed to know who he was? What a great impression I must have made!*

Speaking of first impressions, I'll never forget when I first met you, Elizabeth. It was at that training seminar for teaching special needs children and you were assigned to be my mentor for the week. Lucky me! When you spoke about why you loved teaching so much, I knew we'd be a good match. I'm so lucky to have friends like you and Paul.

I'm starting to fade. Please write and tell me about all the normal stuff. You know, the weather, wildlife, pets, gardening, taking walks, stuff like that.

I miss you guys already.

Giant Hugs,

Jeanne

As my eyes begin to fail on me, I set my two alarm clocks for 4:30 A.M. Fearful of oversleeping, I've brought two alarm clocks just in case one fails. Wanting to change into my pajamas, I walk over to my door to lock it. I turn the lock and it spins with no resistance. *The lock on my door is broken!* I decide to change my clothes in the bathroom. Though I don't like the idea of going to sleep with my door unlocked, I'm too exhausted to worry about it tonight. I turn off the lights and

gaze out the two-by-two-foot square porthole at the sun setting over the Olympic Mountains. Vibrant hues of gold,
orange, pink, red, purple and blue sweep the sky creating a
scene that looks like a surreal painting. It evokes a memory I
have of a picture I've seen of the beautiful fjords in Norway. If
I were a bird and could fly, I'd fly seaward toward the setting
sun, spy mountain goats on Mount Angeles, swoop down over
swimmers in Lake Crescent, breathe in the fresh clean air
from the Olympic National Forest and glide down to the
beach beside the Pacific Ocean on the Makah Indian
Reservation past Neah Bay. Despite ending my night with a
warm smile brought about by this breathtaking view, I have a
restless night. I toss and turn, waking at every sound. I remind
myself over and over that I have begun my new life at sea but
questions and fears crowd in.

Chapter Four

The Voyage Begins

The next morning I awake to the loud, annoying buzzes and screeches of my alarm clocks, feeling as if I didn't sleep at all last night. I quickly get dressed and leave my room. I notice a sign in my passageway that says ENG DEPT. "English Department," I say to myself. Three more steps and it hits me. No, no, no. Engine Department.

I open the stairwell door, which yawls like a cat dipped in water, and tiptoe down one flight of stairs to the crew lounge on A Deck. There, a guy in orange coveralls sleeps sitting up in the semi-darkness. Trying not to startle him, I walk softly across the deserted mess hall to the empty galley, where one dim light burns over the large stainless steel stove. Looking around, I see no sign of my boss.

The crew mess hall serves twenty. There's a coffee station on one wall, a refrigerator, ice machine and drinking fountain on another, and three long tables covered with soiled, dark green tablecloths. The only natural light filters through three small, dirty portholes onto the unswept, yellow tile deck. It smells like a cross between a coffee shop and an oil rig.

I walk down the serving passageway that connects the crew mess to the officers' mess. Twice as large and ten times cleaner than the crew mess, the officers' mess serves only ten officers. A white waxed tiled floor and six portholes the size of picture windows greet the officers at every meal. Instead of three long tables, it has one long table and two round tables covered with starched, pressed, white tablecloths, one filled with snacks: Ritz crackers, Oreos, chocolate chip cookies and a bowl of fruit.

I hear some clanging noises back in the crew mess. The guy who was sleeping when I first walked in is now awake and, from the aroma wafting toward me, he's making a pot of coffee. He walks down the passageway and introduces himself. "My name is Robby. I'm a DEU." DEU? That is a rank I didn't hear about in the union hall. Robby explains that it stands for Deck, Engine and Utility, because he works in each department. "I clean the lower half of the house, everything below the galley, while you clean the upper half, D and C Deck passageways and stairwells, the galley, both mess halls and ten officers' rooms. In port, I also help with the lines." He smiles.

Only about two inches taller than me, Robby has a solid build paired somewhat incongruously with a face of baby smooth skin and high cheek bones. Though he looks strong, there's a gentle air of vulnerability about Robby that makes him seem approachable. He smells like the earth.

"Could you show me how to make the coffee?" I ask.

"It's easy as one, two, three. I already started it on the crew side. Come, I'll show you on the officers' side," he says.

Robby dumps seven heaping scoops of ground coffee into the filter lined basket and then pours a pot of cold water through the metal grate above. Turning toward me, Robby looks me square in the face.

"See, told ya. Easy. By the way, the steward getting on, he's a good guy. You're lucky to get him and not the one who just got off. Whew. Lazy. Never baked. Messy and dirty. Rich, the new steward, he's usually down by now, but his wife slept over last night," he says with a wink.

I nod.

"Nothing for you to do except drink a little coffee until Rich comes down."

Coffee? Not on this empty, nerve-racked stomach, I think.

Robby leans forward. "You look nervous. Don't be. No need to be."

"Well, maybe I am a little," I say, my stomach churning.

"If you need help with anything, ask me. We have same jobs, same mops, buckets and cleaning supplies." He laughs jovially as he walks away with the grace of a yoga instructor. Not exactly my idea of a rough, tough sailor. I'm pleasantly surprised.

Rich, my boss and chief steward, strides into the crew mess at 5:00 A.M. humming a Van Morrison tune. He's a country boy with that freshly starched and pressed look, wearing khaki pants and a white, double-breasted, stand-up collared, short-sleeved steward top. At first glance his short white hair makes him look old, but very few wrinkles line his fair-skinned face which turns deep red when he first sees me. He stops abruptly beside the drinking fountain. My guess is no one has told him about me. This ship hasn't had a woman on board for over two years.

"Good morning," I greet him. "I'm Jeanne. The new steward assistant."

After a moment of scratching his head and looking around the room he regains his composure and asks, "Ever sailed before?"

"No," I admit. "This is my first ship."

"Coming up the Haws Pipe, huh?"

"Haws Pipe?" I ask.

"It's how we say starting at the bottom and working your way up. Don't ask me why it's called the Haws Pipe. Probably something to do with where the anchor chain comes up. Started the same way myself. You know, you've got the hardest job on the ship." He scuffs his feet on the soiled deck. "Two people used to do the work you'll be doing alone. You'll be all over this place doing one thing or another. It's a lot to remember in one day, so for today and tomorrow, we'll take it one duty at a time."

"Okay," I say.

"And I gotta tell you one more thing. I just got on last night too and found out the dishwasher's broken. Don't know why 'cause they've been sitting here in port for a week. Seems like anything that needed fixing could have been fixed. But what that's gonna mean for you is a lot more work. We'll have to sterilize those dishes in the third sink, and believe me when I say it's a royal pain. I've done it before.

"Be down here every morning by five, mop both mess halls and this passageway between them." He looks down at the filthy deck. "The guy before you wasn't known for being a hard worker. I suspect you'll have some cleaning up to do after Marty."

"I have his old room," I say. "I understand completely."

"Oh, and one more thing. There are three of us in the steward department. You, me and the chief cook. You know you answer to me and not to the cook, right? Catch my drift?" He scratches his white eyebrow.

I nod my head in understanding.

I roll the mop bucket from the cleaning closet into the officers' mess and begin to clean the floor. The crew mess takes the better part of the hour. Heavy mop. Grungy deck. By the time I finish, sweat's rolling down into my bra. There's something satisfying about physical work, an instant gratification at seeing something dirty and spoiled suddenly become clean and renewed before my eyes. It's the transformation process at the end that makes it so rewarding. Contented, I place the last chair under the third long table just as Rich comes back in to check on my progress.

"That's plenty good for these boys," Rich says. "Come into the galley and I'll show you where to empty the bucket."

He points to a drain located directly under a large copper pot used for cooking pasta. "We use this because the drain in the mop closet is plugged."

I can't help but notice that a lot of things on this ship need repair. Plugged drains, chipped paint, doors that don't lock. Looks like a broken down antique home to me, but I have nothing with which to compare it.

Rich shows me what is needed on each table for breakfast: water and juice pitchers, butter and margarine. He tells me to make a fresh pot of coffee on both sides before each meal. When I'm finished doing that, I come back into the galley.

Rich's wife, a beautiful raven-haired woman, must have walked into the galley as Rich was explaining everything to me. She sits beside the brown plastic trays and silverware. She's as dark as Rich is light. Burnt sienna skin, piercing brown eyes and a smile that makes me happy just to see it.

We nod at each other and when I look at Rich for an intro
duction but get none, I introduce myself.

"Hi. I'm Jeanne."

"I'm Carmen. I drove my husband here last night
and slept over," she speaks in a sugary contralto voice and
smiles enigmatically.

"It must be hard to say good-bye for four months," I
say.

"Oh, we don't wait four months to see each other.
When the ship docks in a Washington port, I drive to the
coast to meet up with it. It depends on which captain is on,
but most of them let wives spend the night on the ship when
it's docked in a port."

"No time for girl talk now," Rich interrupts. "Breakfast
starts at seven. Time to clean a room or two. Start with the
second engineer's and the second mate's. They pull the four
to eight watch, so if they're in their bunks, they shouldn't be."

I walk up to C Deck. It is empty and quiet. I tiptoe around
until I find the second engineer's room with its door slightly
ajar. I knock. No answer. The thought of going into a stranger's
room in which I'll have to touch and move things to clean
feels weird. I hate the idea of prying into a person's private
space when the person is not there. Even worse, what if the
person is there—changing his clothes or sleeping? I knock
again, still no answer. Finally, I push the door open further and

peek inside to find the second engineer's room is vacant. He has three framed photos of his wife and children on his desk directly below giant posters of scantily clad girls. One's a Dallas Cowboy cheerleader and the other's an exotic island girl with long dark hair covering bare breasts. I wonder how his wife would feel about being stationed beneath them.

I look over the room in disbelief. *Someone is actually living in here.* A greasy inch of dust covers every flat surface. Dust bunnies rule the floors and corners. I'm afraid to look in the bathroom. It's clearly an overwhelming situation, so I immediately make a plan for all the rooms. Day one: make the beds and sweep up the big chunks of collected dirt and debris. Day two: dust. Day three: toilets. Day four: showers. Day five: mop.

The second mate's room on D Deck is lit only by the dim bathroom light, and although I hope for the best, it's hopelessly dirtier. Here, however, bags of red licorice replace the pin-up girls. It's a veritable red-vine garden.

After sweeping the two rooms, I return to the galley for breakfast and find Rich stirring pancake batter. He looks at me from the corner of his eye. "So, what's the situation up there?"

"Gross is one of many words that comes to mind," I say.

"Yep. Uh hunh. That's Marty. Well, spread the wealth. Don't go trying to conquer Rome in a day. The boys tell me that Marty's style was to walk in, flush the toilet and spray air freshener."

"No doubt," I mutter.

"You hungry? 'Cause if you are, you'd better eat now before all those boys get down here and the dishes start flying in. What's your fancy? I cook to order."

"Two eggs scrambled with cheese, please," I say.

"Okay, now fix up your plate with whatever else you want and by the time you've got your juice, fruit and muffin, I'll have those eggs good and ready."

In less than a minute he calls, "Order's up, Jeanne. Now take those beauties into the crew mess and sit a minute while you eat. I guarantee ya it'll be your only time to relax until after lunch."

The crew mess is empty but for one older guy. I sit down across from him.

"I'm Stanley," he gives me a broad smile. He tells me he's been in shipping since he was seventeen and now he's the oldest AB on the ship—in his sixties. A Swede, Stanley smells like Old Spice and looks like the old farmer husband holding the pitch fork in Grant Wood's famous painting, *American Gothic*. He seems like a man for whom the decades of routine ship life have been his salvation; a man who would crumble if forced to sit behind a desk in a suit and tie for thirty years. But I can see he is also a man whose body is protesting, at last, from years and years of hard, manual labor. When he lifts his spoon to his mouth, every now and again his hand quivers.

"None of these guys like me, because I won't work overtime," Stanley says.

In my mind I hear Fred York yakking on and on about how the first eight hours on a ship are just the appetizer, how everyone works close to twelve hours a day. And here sits Stanley, who day after week after month after year after decade has worked twelve-hour days, going home to his wife for the occasional respite, then back again to his prison-like tanker cell for another four-month gig. Now Stanley is tired.

By this time, other guys are sitting down to eat. Headed to the chow line, a few officers walk through the crew mess and not one walks past without breaking his neck doing a double take of me.

"The overtime hours aren't in our union contracts," Stanley continues.

Theoretically, there is nothing anyone can do to him. Except to ostracize him, which seems to be the case.

"Excuse me, Stanley. Time's up for me. I hear dishes hitting the pass-through window." So ends my only rest break between five in the morning and two in the afternoon.

In the middle of breakfast while Rich cooks and I wash dishes, in walks a large man in his mid-forties with a red bulbous nose. He wears sloppy, food-stained khakis and a grease-stained T-shirt. He looks like the distant uncle who comes to visit once a year, drinks great quantities of cheap beer, then asks unsuspecting victims to pull his finger so he can release a fart.

"So we finally get Marty off the ship and they send us this?" The new guy nods in my direction from the doorway, hands on his hips.

Rich introduces me to Al, the chief cook.

"I hope you know what you're in for," Al says, lips curled.

"I think I have a pretty good idea," I say with the best attitude voice I can muster.

"This is my work space. I don't want anything set down here—ever." With his pudgy hands Al motions to the countertop to the right of the three sinks and pushes a tray of dirty dishes off the counter into the soapy water. He turns and reaches for something in one of the overhead cupboards and his dirty green T-shirt rises up above his waist exposing his sagging pants and the top of his butt crack. After seeing that sight, the sink full of dirty dishes looks like stars twinkling on a clear night.

Five trays come in at once. Rich grabs two, I catch the next two. Rich nabs the last one.

"Well now, aren't you two the little dream team. Coffee time for the cook," All says without lifting a finger and walks out.

I laugh a nervous giggle.

"Laugh now 'cause if the cook ever gets his hooks on you, you won't be laughing. No sir. No siree," Rich says.

Carmen, who will leave the ship after breakfast, gives Rich a big smile, and I imagine the two of them dancing.

She throws her head back and laughs, "We are happy people, you and me, si?"

And Rich answers, "Si, senora," mumbling "Quick, quick, slow, quick, quick, slow."

I try to find a rhythm, but the workload's more than I ever imagined. Every job involves lifting, dragging, pushing or pulling something incredibly heavy. But what puts me over the edge is the broken dishwasher. The galley has three sinks, and if the dishwasher worked, my job would be to rinse and scrape the dishes in the sink on the right, wash and rinse them in the middle sink, then place them in the dishwasher for sterilization. But since its broken, my job has changed. In Rich's new system, I rinse and scrape the dishes in the right sink, wash and rinse them in the middle sink, then place them in the left sink, which Rich fills with scalding water from the pasta machine. Strange. After the dishes have been in the scalding water for at least two minutes, I remove them with tongs while wearing heavy-duty rubber gloves so as not to get scalded. I repeat lifting out of the sink each plate, platter, glass, saucer, cup, pot and pan with the tongs. It quickly begins to takes its toll. I can barely see what I am holding in front of me because of the steam rising in my face. It burns my arms so I try switching back and forth between my left hand and my right hand whenever one starts to hurt too much. I hope they get the dishwasher fixed soon. I'm not sure I can do dishes like this for a crew of thirty people, three times a day, for sixty days. It's killing me already just thinking about it.

Even though I've always been physically fit—chopped wood, lifted weights, ridden my bike over mountain passes—I never once thought about being unable to keep up with any kind of manual work. I tell myself it's probably just a period of adjustment, getting used to twelve-hour days, the stress of change and perhaps not getting enough sleep. I try hard not to worry about it and focus more on the task at hand.

Whenever I get caught up, dirty dish trays magically appear in the pass-through window, and they rarely come one at a time. When one tray gets shoved through the stainless steel pass-through, others follow. It's a nightmare. Sometimes I feel like Lucy and Ethel in the candy factory when the assembly line of chocolates accelerates and they can't keep up. If I don't make it to the pass-through in time to pick up a dirty tray, some guys are considerate enough to help out a little. Others plunk down their tray on top of the first one without a care as to dishes breaking or food spilling on the deck.

Despite the heavy tasks, Rich and I are a team. If I'm elbow deep in dishwater, he's right there picking up extra trays. He can cook six or seven breakfast orders at a time and still help me out in between.

Breakfast is his element. He likes looking up from the grill to see another guy on the chow line, and he has nicknames for several crew members, some of which he uses in their presence, and others he'll only use in front of me after they have walked away.

Coming up to the line is Todd, the chief pumpman. Rich calls him "Sugar" because Todd claims to be diabetic and only able to eat certain things, yet he comes through the chow line and piles so much of everything on his tray that it sags in the middle. A funny, jovial man with a round face and plump cheeks, Sugar eats all of his food mixed up in a big bowl. I know it's bad to joke about people, but I love his nickname. It makes me laugh and I'm quickly learning we need to laugh with this burden of work.

As for lunch and dinner, Rich takes care of the salad bar and desserts; everything else needed for those two meals are the domain of Al, the chief cook. I'd never let him know that he scares me, but he does. And I have to work with him in the galley every single day. I tell myself that I won't stoop to his level. I'll be professional no matter what—professional and distant. That is the plan.

As the day goes on, I count the number of times that I run up and down the four flights from A Deck to D Deck:

thirty-two. I get tired of going up and down, but it makes for a great quadriceps workout. I'm still not sure which rooms are empty at what times, but I have been getting to know some of the crew by knocking on their door when they're inside. At least I am working on my positive thinking skills.

A mate runs toward me in the stairwell. I smell him five steps away: Aramis. It smells great. "Hey, thanks for making my bed," he says.

"You're welcome," I reply. "Which room is yours?"

"I'm Third Mate Stanton. Call me Pete."

He's in his late twenties. Really cute with sparkling blue eyes, jet black hair and a boyish smile. He reminds me of Tom Cruise. At this point he's the only mate who's taken the time to say hello while walking past me. Apparently, the majority of them take the non-fraternization guideline pretty seriously.

He jumps past me, taking the stairs three steps at a time, all the while holding the hand rails.

On my blessed hour-and-a-half afternoon break I walk out on deck to look at the port and city. It's a perfect 75 degrees. I face southwest and gaze at the majestic Olympic Mountains. They tower over waterways surrounded by lush forests. I've hiked the trails of Mt. Olympus when wild trillium covered whole hillsides. Even on the trails, my boots soaked through from water rolling off the thick growth of fern fronds. I turn back to the Strait of Juan de Fuca to contemplate the watery trails that lie ahead of me. The city of Victoria, across the straight, glitters in the sun.

While strolling on the deck outside, I pass the first mate who Rich calls "Smiley," because he does the exact opposite—he never smiles. Rich explains that it's because he's from Alaska and they only have one day of summer, but I think maybe he had some traumatic experience that took away his ability to take pleasure in being happy. Then again, maybe not smiling is what makes him happy. Smiley smells like burnt toast and hides porn magazines under his mattress. I saw them when I tucked his messy covers and bedspread under the foot of his bed. "Where's your hard hat?" he yells.

I place my hand on top of my head as if I thought it were there, but I know I left it in my room. "I, ah, I left it inside."

He yells at me again for not wearing a hard hat and explains the dangers of not following the rule. Several guys on deck are also hatless, but since it's my first day, I feel I cannot tell him this. To avoid any further tongue lashings, I trudge back up to my room and put on my stupid orange hard hat.

Smiley has only spoken to me twice. Once to bark a request from his room, "Hey! Think you could spare a couple boxes of Kleenex?" and the other to yell at me about the damn hardhat. I begin to wonder if he's like this with everyone or if he just has a problem with me.

I return to the deck to continue my jaunt when I realize that there are two tugboats in the water next to the ship. There's one tug on each side of the ship. I lean over the railing to have a better look. I hear footsteps behind me and when I turn around, I see Pete approaching me in his white coveralls and orange hard hat. Even in that get-up he still looks cute. He seems like the kind of person who just always does the right thing naturally.

I ask him about the two tugs.

"They're escorting us out of the harbor in case something happens and we need help," he explains. "Oil spills and all that." Then he looks me up and down quickly. "Is this your first sail?"

"Yes. Before getting on this ship I taught English at a college."

"Get the hell outta here!" he says, kicking the railing. He looks around and whispers, "Don't be surprised if you get shit for walking out here on the deck."

"I already did. What's the deal?"

He shakes his head. "Hard to explain with you being new to shipping and all, but ships are just structured that way, you know? To not be friendly."

"You heard him yell at me earlier, didn't you?" I tuck stray pieces of my wind-blown hair up into the hard hat.

Pete looks out at the tug chugging away next to us but doesn't answer.

"It's kind of like the military, I guess, where certain groups don't fraternize with the others," I observe.

He smiles at me, a little sadly. "Yeah and you're the woman group," he says, lowering his voice again. "Don't tell anyone what I said, okay?"

I finish my dinner duties by 6:30 P.M. Having a little spare time I climb the outside stairs to B Deck, take the clip out of my hair, and let the wind blow through it. I breathe in the salty sea breeze as it brushes gently against my face. We can still see land tonight but by morning it will be only water. I can feel my chest tighten slightly; I am both excited and sad about that idea. I love the land and I love the sea. I am also worried that seeing the endless horizon of blue sky meeting the deep blue sea will get monotonous without the disruption land offers. It shouldn't be too bad though as long as I keep reminding myself that I am living my dream.

After a few peaceful moments with nature I walk back to my room. I look again at the broken lock on my door in annoyance. *I really have to do something about this*, I think. I experiment to see what I can do to fix the problem and finally figure out that if I prop the metal chair from my desk between my room door and the closet door, the outer door will be jammed shut. I do this and then peel off my sweaty galley clothes. It's going to be my daily routine: Strip off clothes, shower and wash hair twice to get rid of the stench. I towel off and smudge myself from top to bottom with incense smoke, then place the incense stick in its holder in the sink. Smudging is a Native American process for spiritual purification. The smoke from the incense is supposed to carry off negative energy. Spiritual renewal and the release of negative energy—both are things I'm in need of right now.

I don sweats for the walk that I promise I will try to take every evening, weather permitting of course. Then I change my mind. I have already been on the deck twice today and I'm too damned tired. Cleaning ten officers' rooms, mopping passageways and stairwells, setting up and tearing down mess halls, washing three meals of dishes by hand will wear anyone out, especially on the first day. I feel like a homesick kid at a miserable summer camp counting the days until I get to leave. Only fifty-nine left.

With my head resting now on the pillow, I lie on the bunk and listen to the engine from deep in the belly of the ship. I hear its rhythm like a heartbeat and feel its cadence under me. Raising myself on one elbow, I stare out at the view from my porthole. The moon has an orange glow like the summer sun and casts its light onto the snow-covered Olympic Mountains. The distant landscape is so perfect it looks surreal. Even after the long day of hard work, I tell myself that seeing such beauty will help me relax, fall asleep and have a dream-filled, restful night. At least I hope so.

Chapter Five

Advanced Swimming Lessons

"Did I smell incense last night?" Rich asks at breakfast while he flips blueberry pancakes.

"Yes. I smudge," I say, waiting for the strange look and the inevitable questions, but Rich surprises me.

"My wife smudges, too. Just be careful with it," he warns. "This is an oil tanker, you know."

The scent of buttery sweet pancakes makes me feel hungry again. "I burn it in the sink," I say.

"Sounds good." He nods and chuckles as he changes the subject. "Cleaned the captain's room yet?"

"No, yesterday he said he didn't want to be disturbed while leaving port."

"Every captain has different ways," Rich says. "See which way he blows after breakfast. Address him as either 'sir' or 'captain.'"

Serving breakfast and cleaning the dishes takes on much of the same chaos as it did yesterday. Rich and I juggle the trays in order to sanitize them in the scalding water. I am surprised that I have not burnt myself that badly yet.

When the dishes are all clean, I walk up the four flights of stairs, wondering how my assigned tasks will go. The first thing I have to do is speak with the captain. I knock on his open office door.

"Good morning, sir," I say as cheerfully as I can muster.

Captain Figarino barely looks up from his papers as I walk through his office into his bedroom with my bucket of cleaning supplies. While dusting, I overhear him talking on the phone. It must be his wife or one of his kids, I surmise, because he sounds like a pussycat. At the end of his conversation he lowers his voice and says a hushed, "Bye-bye," as sweet as pie.

I've only seen two expressions on his face: smiling and scowling. When he scowls, it's as if the ship herself tightens her boiler and runs. I know he's married with three kids, but the scuttlebutt is that he's having an affair with a Valdez official. I don't know if it's true or not. But if it is, he'll be in a hurry to get there, so we'll make good time.

On my way out I notice the scowling look is back on his face.

I try to be diplomatic. "Sir, do you have a preference as to when I clean your room?"

"Breakfast. 7:30. Maybe a little after," he mumbles.

"Very good sir." I edge out of the room and I'm halfway down the passageway when Figarino calls out my name.

"And, Jeanne?"

"Sir?" I walk back to his open door.

"Come back up here at one this afternoon and we'll get you signed in."

"Very good, sir," I reply and go on to tackle my remaining duties.

My next room assignment is that of Chief Engineer Scruggs which is directly below the captain's office. Scruggs is also sitting at his desk when I knock on the open door to his office, which is identical to the captain's office. He doesn't have girly calendars in his room, no pin-ups on the walls like some of the other members of our crew do. His wife's photo is on his bedside table next to a book about fly-fishing. When it comes to having his room cleaned, Scruggs is the exact opposite of Figarino. He's much more relaxed.

"Set your own schedule. As long as that door is open, it's all yours," he says. Yet, paradoxically, he's an economy of language kind of guy. Fast. Efficient. So far Scruggs seems like an authentic, down to earth man.

I start to work on formulating a daily schedule of the order in which I will clean the rooms. I get through my chores much faster than yesterday and am content with how quickly I am adjusting to this new job.

At lunch I sit across from Stanley, the oldest crew-member, again. I eat early to get a headstart on the dirty dishes. Stanley eats early to avoid the other guys.

"Well, I'm still here and will be tomorrow, the good Lord willing," Stanley sighs as he finishes his pot roast and gravy.

"You know," he leans closer to me, "the American Indians, when they wanted to kill an enemy, why, they'd catch a poisonous snake and put it in a jar with an article of clothing from their enemy. After that snake'd been in there a few days and was meaner than snot, they'd take that jar and open it in the enemy's camp at night. Boy howdy, if that snake didn't hate the guy who the shirt belonged to." He nods his head, his narrowed eyes deepening the creases in his wrinkled face. "I know just how that snake felt," he whispers.

I wonder exactly who it is that Stanley hates. I wonder too, what might have been the jar in my father's life. When Stanley leaves the table I walk over to Rich and start to prepare myself for the onslaught of lunch's dirty dishes.

"How come none of the guys like Stanley?" I ask Rich back in the galley.

"Overtime issue. Too much to do and not enough hands to do it. Before the crew cutbacks, two people carried the load of my job, and in addition to the cook and steward, we had a pastry chef. We're a bare-bones crew now, so everyone works eleven to twelve hours a day. Everyone except Stanley."

In a way I admire Stanley for taking a stance about overtime. He's older and he conserves his energy that way. It's not in his contract. But then again, it's not fair to the rest of the crew.

As I wash the brown plastic trays, I begin to notice interesting patterns that form when I lift them out of the scalding rinse water. The swirling, free-form patterns look like melted oak leaves in a Salvador Dali painting until the trays dry completely and shift back to plain old, ordinary brown plastic. A very Zen moment in what I can already be assured will be a very long day.

Rich walks over to the sink to add more hot water, and I make the mistake of showing him the patterns on the tray. He looks puzzled, steps back. "Well now. Smoked a little too much weed back in the seventies, huh?"

We joke around as we clean all the dishes and trays. Time seems to fly as long as we are laughing with one another. Before I know it, it's one o'clock. I leave the galley and climb the four flights of stairs up to the captain's cabin. Figarino sees me before my knuckles hit his open door.

"Come in. Come in," he calls out. "I need to know how you want to be paid. Every week? Every two weeks? A stipend when we're close to port and the remainder in a check at the end of your sixty days? What would you like?"

"Sir, I'd like one big check on my last day."

He looks puzzled. "No spending money in ports?"

"No thanks. My debit card will cover that."

"You sure?" he asks uncertainly.

"I'm sure."

He looks closer at me and asks, "What were you doing before this?"

"I taught at a college."

"What did you teach?" he presses, his curiosity piqued.

"English courses: composition, creative writing, literature, humanities."

"And now you're doing this for us?" he asks, looking over his shoulder toward his room.

I raise my chin slightly. "Yes."

"But—that's crazy. Surely you must have made a better wage working there than here."

"Actually, sir," I confess, "I was only making roughly $1200 a month."

He stares at me incredulously. A rosy hue begins at his throat zips up his neck and blooms on his cheeks. "That's despicable," he nearly spits out. "There's plenty of guys without even high school diplomas making a great deal more than that on ships."

Shrugging my shoulders, I respond, "I know sir. I guess it's just the luck of the draw."

"Well, Jeanne. You'll make good money on this ship. You'll get your one big paycheck just as you requested."

"Thank you, sir," I respond and take my leave.

I'm tidying up the mess halls before my afternoon break when Pete, the stair-jumping third mate and fellow deck-walker finds me. I like him. His room is messy but clean. Yes, there are clothes tossed around, but no unflushed toilet or a bunch of gross toothpaste lumps mixed with whiskers in the sink. A photo of his fiancee sits proudly on the nightstand next to a calendar with his sail days crossed off.

He taps me on the shoulder. "Captain wants me to go over safety rules and regulations with you."

He starts in on what the different ship whistles mean, policies on alcohol, drugs and dumping trash overboard and all I can think about is the fact that my feet feel like they belong to a prehistoric animal. I want nothing more than to be in my room, lying on my bunk with a masseuse rubbing my feet.

"Pete, I need to sit down," I say, so we sit at the table closest to the coffee station while he coaches me for fifteen precious minutes of my break.

"Okay, now tell me where you'd go in case of a fire?" he asks.

Depends on whether or not I've had my nap, I feel like saying but I answer it straight. "To the passageway across from the medical office on the upper deck."

He nods. "Good. Now what blasts would you hear if there were a fire?"

I must have been sleeping during that part of the lecture, so I guess six short and one long.

He shakes his head no. "Well, you had a fifty-fifty chance of getting it right but you got it wrong. Okay, try to focus. What's happening and where do you go if you hear this: Hm, hm, hm, hm, hm, hm, hmmmmmmm?"

I throw back my head and laugh. I can't help it, but Pete just stares at me; he wants an answer. I regain my composure and think for a moment when it suddenly comes to me. "Okay, I know. Man overboard. Go to my lifeboat, port side."

He's happy now, but only for a second. "Right, but explain to me what's happening and where you go if you hear one long, deep blast, **HMMMMMMM!**

"Right, I remember now. That's the sign that there's a fire. I'd go to the passageway across from the medical office on upper deck."

Pete nods his head, satisfied. The quiz is over. I passed. I practically float up to my room. I lie on my bunk, leave my feet dangling in the air and press an ice pack between my tired hands. It is not even a moment after I close my eyes that one long, continuous ship blast shrieks through the air. 'Fire drill' is the answer that enters my mind for this twisted pop quiz.

I stumble into my pants, shirt and shoes, grab my life vest and hat, then scramble out the door with the other sleepy-eyed mariners who are fumbling over their shirt buttons and trying to tie their shoes. Everyone except for the captain assembles for the fire drill. The first mate, Smiley, who yelled at me for walking on deck without a hard hat, is in charge. He's frowning while he talks to the captain who's giving him orders from the bridge. Every now and then, Smiley shakes his head and looks more unhappy than usual. Only God knows what the captain says that makes Smiley bark orders loudly and breathe fire from his nostrils. At this point he has everyone jumping in one direction or another. No one is happy, because fire drills are usually scheduled. Everyone usually knows when they're going to happen, but only Figarino and Smiley knew about this one. Sneaky. It throws everybody off schedule and puts people in bad moods. Rich and Al are especially cranky, because they're losing most of their food preparation time.

I'm so tired that I feel like dozing off during the drill. All I know is that my lifeboat is on port side and my fire buddies are the galley guys, Robby, Pete and a cute guy named Steve. Robby tells me that Steve is the bosun, which is short for boatswain, the ship's petty officer in charge of the entire deck crew. I also notice that a couple guys smile when they look at me.

"You're the only woman on an all male ship. Of course they're smiling at you," Rich says when I mention it to him while we pretend to put out a fire.

What's left of my break when the fire drill ends passes too quickly. All I have time to do is get back to my room, lie on my bed for a few moments and curse the drill.

I slip begrudgingly back into my heavy, steel-toed boots, put my hair up in a clip and brush my teeth. The rest of the day and night passes uneventfully.

Water soaked, I walk into the galley early the next morning.

"Well don't you look like something the cat dragged in," Rich says.

I massage my left forearm. "I've been cleaning showers."

"Whooee, whoeee! You've got a lot to learn." Now he gets excited. He loves sharing secret cleaning tips. "You want to save yourself some hard work? Forget about regular cleaners. You put some of that floor stripper in a spray bottle and spray those shower walls. Then you just watch that soap scum slide right off. No need to scrub. Just be sure to rinse," he says.

"Really?"

"You betcha."

"How could I have raised two kids and not know how to clean a shower?" I ask.

He winks. "Because now you're talking to an old pro. Now, how are you doing with making up those bunks?"

"I get lumps no matter what I do," I run my hand through my hair. "It's awkward, the way the mattress is wedged between three walls."

"Make it easy on yourself. Lift that mattress up on the open side in front of you, then pull everything—sheet, blanket and spread—underneath the mattress toward you, nice and tight. Those boys won't be messing up those covers for a week." He smiles like a man without a care in the world.

Breakfast goes smoothly once again and I am slowly figuring out how to do my morning chores. I don't have the schedule set yet, but I am getting closer with each passing day. Lunch, on the other hand, is a whole different matter.

"There's some soap on that last pan," the cook calls out at lunch. He's been watching my every move for twenty minutes and thinks I haven't noticed.

I'd like to tell him to take a flying leap. Instead I take one long, deep breath. I try everything to keep my lips zipped: deep breaths, counting to ten in my mind and simply ignoring him. I keep reminding myself to remain professional yet distant. Professional, yet distant.

A short while later I round the corner to the galley broom closet and there stands beautiful Robby, face shiny with goodwill. He points to the new supplies on the lowest shelf: an extra bottle of Simple Green and a new mop head. "Hope these will make your job easier," he offers. I am left speechless. Who is this kind man?

I begin my afternoon tasks moving slower than usual. I remember being filled with energy and ready to clean and complete my tasks only days ago when I first started this endeavor. It seems like an eternity has passed since then.

My legs and arms get heavier as today slowly passes. The fatigue that has been setting in is worse than jet lag. I never feel rested. It's always like I just woke up and haven't had my first cup of coffee for the day. Between the lead weight of my exhausted body and the slow, rhythmic motion of the ship, my thoughts begin to wander. I think of childhood summers with Mom and Grandma, two strong women who helped make me the person I am today...

Acting like a young girl that day, Mom had packed egg salad sandwiches in a basket with fresh peaches and a quart jar of milk for a day out fishing. I watched her walk with her yellow house dress swaying as she bounced over rocks down by the river. She was singing, "Camptown ladies sing this song, doo-dah, doo-dah." I wanted to run and place my hand in hers, but I didn't for fear of breaking the magic spell that was cast over that perfect day.

Mom, my older sister and I fished for the better part of the morning. We shared two poles and watched the red bobbers float in the sunlight. Mom handed me the pole then waded into the moving water. I took my eyes off the bobber and watched her as she made her way downstream. I watched as she removed her shoes and nylon stockings then submerged her smooth, alabaster legs, one at a time, into the gurgling water.

Suddenly the pole shifted in my hands. I grabbed it tightly and my sister hollered, "She's got one! Jeanne's got one." Mom sprinted back to the bridge as I clung to the fishing pole with all my might. I wanted that fish. I wanted more than anything to please my mother.

"I've got one!" I yelled.

"You sure as hell do," my mom said as she grabbed the pole and pulled with me, laughing until a big catfish finally shot up out of the water. I touched the whiskered fish as it flapped side-to-side on the bridge. When my mother hugged me tight, I wanted time to stop right there. It was the first hug from her that I could remember. I was four years old and wanted it to always be like this.

Grandma's wrists were strong from always making homemade bread. I loved watching her knead the dough. It reminded me of watching an artist sculpt. The dough yielded under her hands, conformed to her pulling and stretching. Later, it rose and Grandma punched it down. The sticky white dough collapsed and sighed. She folded it and set it to rise again.

On this particular day Grandma covered the bowl of dough with a clean kitchen towel while she sang "Softly and Tenderly."

"Grandma, how come you sing all the time?" I asked.

She looked at me and chuckled. "I never gave it much thought but I suppose I sing because Jesus put a song in my heart."

"How'd he do that?"

"Well, if you aren't one big question now?" She wiggled the tip of my nose with her pointer finger.

I giggled. "But, how'd he do it?"

"Why Jeanne Marie, he lives in my heart."

"You sure have a lot of things in your heart."

"Now you go sit a spell on the porch swing or we'll never get off on our evening walk."

I went outside and sat on the swing. As I rocked back and forth I tried to decide what I wanted to do with my life. The only answer I could find was that I wanted to be like Grandma. I wanted to be kind and caring just like her. I wanted to do things like make jam, bake my own bread and go for walks with my grandchildren.

It broke my heart when she died a few years later. Her casket was set up in the parlor next to the bay window, her profile visible from the living room and kitchen. I kept expecting her to rise up, straighten her hair and ask for help to get out of the casket so she could start cooking dinner.

Although she lay in the parlor for four days straight, I couldn't get used to seeing her like that—motionless, lifeless. She meant so much to me, I never wanted to let her go.

Finally finished with my afternoon duties, I take a walk out on the deck to get some fresh air. The warm Alaskan summer sun hangs in the sky, but I know it won't set for a couple of hours. I look down at the dark blue water glistening with shades of gold, orange and crimson. The sea is a little choppy and the breeze is strong, but when I look off in the distance the water appears flat and unmoving. The line where the warm sky meets the cold, dark water is a slight arc, smooth and endless. I survey the scene and realize how small I am in this world. There are no passing ships, no signs of life. Out here it's just this tanker with twenty-nine men and one woman cruising on the vast open ocean toward Valdez, Alaska.

According to Stanley, we're six or seven hundred miles from land, too far for a helicopter to race out and give us a helping hand in an emergency. Not the kind of information I'll share with my kids. I look straight down at the cold, dark water below and wonder what it would be like to fall overboard and be left behind out here. I wonder what it would feel like to drown. I've come close a couple times, close enough to know I don't want to die that way.

When I was five, before I could swim, I tagged along with my nine-year-old sister to the town pool. Other kids jumped off the edge into the water, and although she offered to catch me several times, I wouldn't do it; like all big sisters she'd played too many tricks on me. Instead, I sat in a sun-warmed puddle on the cement at the shallow end of the pool, watching the other kids. Finally, my sister swam down to the deep end to play with her friends.

Feeling left out, I got up and stood at the edge of the pool. I looked down into the water, blurred by kicking feet, windmill arms and glinting sunlight, then took that giant step forward. I felt my feet land on the bottom of the pool, but no matter how hard I bobbed up and down, water covered my head. I kept my eyes open, saw other kid's shoulders, stomachs, feet and arms, but no faces. I held my breath as long as I could while I bobbed toward the side of the pool but never reached it. When I couldn't hold my breath any longer, I breathed in, and the pain of breathing in the water panicked me. The more I panicked, the more I breathed in. I think that's what drowning would feel like all the way to the end, until you quit struggling.

That's when I was rescued. An older girl grabbed me up out of the water and asked if I was okay.

Then all the lifeguards rushed over. I threw up and cried, and when they let me sit up, I looked around for the big girl. I wanted to give her a huge hug and thank her, because I knew that if she hadn't lifted me up, I'd be dead. Before the commotion ended and the crowd thinned, my sister saw me in the center of it all. She came over quickly and rushed me home immediately. I never found the big girl to say thank you. When I told the story to my grandma that night, I told her that an angel picked me up out of the water and put me on the concrete at the side of the pool.

One day, the following week, my dad milked the cows in the morning, came in for lunch as usual, but instead of going out to work in the field after lunch, he changed into town clothes and told me we were driving to the town pool. I was so nervous about going back there I had to bite my lip hard to keep back the tears.

He gripped my hand tightly and pulled me into the pool office. "This little gal wants to sign up for beginner swimming lessons next week," he said.

I'm six hundred miles from shore with thoughts of drowning and memories of my dad. He had some loving traits and, as in the case of the swimming lessons, he occasionally did "fatherly" things that showed he cared about my safety and well-being. But the cruel treatment I suffered at his hands always blots out the few good things I can remember. I rub my aching forehead and close my eyes. I'm too tired to think about it all right now, so I push the past back into its place.

My break is over. I head to the galley for dinner duties. After dinner, I encounter Steve, the bosun, in the laundry room where I put a load of work clothes in the washing machine. As I pour the soap into the washer, I try to act nonchalant and not stare at him, but it's difficult. He's undoubtedly the most handsome man I've ever met. Even in goggles and a hardhat, he's attractive. French Creole, Steve has long, dark brown hair in a ponytail that reaches to his waist. He's easy to talk with, a very sweet man. Even as I chat with him, I'm struck again by his good looks. He talks about his home, his wife, how they met while shipping together.

When I'm done with the laundry, I leave and walk toward the bow on starboard side. The deck is tipsy under my feet. The wind has really picked up since this afternoon. Huge waves slap against the sides of the ship. I make it to the bow, an oasis, where I listen to the roaring sound of the big swells as they hit the steel hull. Every time the bow dips down after cresting, it sounds like waves crashing on a beach. I close my eyes and imagine myself on an exotic island like Bora Bora. For several minutes I stand there and envision myself lying on warm sand listening to the crashing surf.

But when I head back toward the house on port side, my serenity is interrupted by the swells crashing over the rail as the bow dips into a roller. Salt water showers over me as well. I am knocked off my feet by the force of the breaker. Frightened and embarrassed, I scramble starboard and see that Steve is running toward me.

"Hey. Should have told you we were taking on water port side. It's too dangerous to walk on the wind side in big swells like this. Any rougher and we close the decks. You fall in and the water's so cold most people only last about ten minutes. It would take us longer than that to turn this baby around."

He walks with me. The wind whips our hair and clothes. I've always loved wind. Maybe because it does what it wants when it wants. Maybe I wish I could be like that: strong, powerful, unafraid, in control, able to do what I want, when I want. I remember how my mother hated the wind when it blew hard, hated how it messed up her coifed and sprayed hair, hated the feeling of it pressing against her, hated the noise it made. Maybe my love for the wind is simply a childish rebellion. Maybe if my mother had loved it, I would hate it, but I really don't think so. Wind is a living presence for me; a companion with whom I fall in love, again and again.

As we walk back toward the stern, the waves break behind us on the bow. The sound of the swells becomes louder and louder as if they will soon crash down on us. Listening to them makes me feel connected to the fierceness of nature. I can feel my heart beat quicken in utter amazement at the sea's strength and glory.

"I've been in fifty-foot swells that are mean enough to rattle even big ships like this one," Steve tells me. "When it gets any rougher than this, you'll need to shove your dry-suit stuff sack under the open side of your mattress to keep from rolling out your bunk. It's a make-shift hammock that's not too comfortable, but better than rolling out onto the deck all night. Maybe check with me before your walks, eh?"

After Steve leaves, I stand outside the door, holding to the rails on the house as I watch a twenty-foot wall of water rise above my head. The swells bend and roll; they rock us, but not gently.

I trod over to the deck hands who are chipping paint on the stern. They smile my way and continue with their tedious scraping. I envy them being outside all day in the fresh air. I envy their freedom to constantly observe the sea, at times serene and peaceful, at other times ferocious and terrifying. I turn port side, but the sight of the water cresting the rails sends me starboard. I don't want to be knocked down again. Once was more than enough. I slowly make my way back to my cabin.

Safe and dry in my room, I lie down for a few moments and revisit in my mind the sight and the feeling of having that wall of water crash down on me. I'm more frightened now about having gone through it than when it happened. What would it feel like to be swept out to sea with less than ten minutes to live? What last thoughts and memories would sweep through my mind in those final moments? I shiver at the thought. I realize the sea is even more powerful and dangerous than I ever imagined. It's a mysterious other world, a black abyss upon which we sail.

Things begin rolling around in my room, so I copy what the officers do in their rooms. I get up and take the piece of rubber padding Robby left beside my door and put some of it under my desk chair. Then I place another piece inside the desk drawer under the pens and pencils. Afterward, I latch the medicine cabinet tight but can't figure out a way to stop the hangers from rattling in the wardrobe. I grab my journal, jump on my bunk and begin writing a letter to my daughters.

At Sea

Dear Lisa and Emily,

It's been a while since I've written so I thought I'd catch you upon on what's been happening. There are some pretty interesting characters out here on the ship. You might even call them "salty." Ha-ha! So far, Robby is my favorite. From the first day, he has gone out of his way to be helpful and very nice to me. He brings me little gifts of cleaning supplies. He's such a sweetheart.

My boss, Rich, is great too. He tells corny jokes, listens to classic rock in the galley and isn't afraid to be goofy. Sometimes he even laughs at my corny jokes! Mostly though, Rich acts as a buffer between Al and me. Al is the chief cook. He's what you could safely call a pain in the butt. A true type-A personality.

Then there's the captain. He's handsome and a fairly complex individual. Just when I think I've got him all figured out, he does something that throws me. For example, he insists that his room be cleaned at a certain time everyday even though it wreaks havoc with my morning schedule. But when I was cleaning it yesterday, he asked me how I was doing and also asked about the two of you. He wanted to know where you live and what you are studying in college. He seemed to take a genuine interest in my life, kind of like an uncle.

Scruggs, our chief engineer, is second in command on the ship. He's a lot more laid back than the captain about when his room is cleaned. He is playful too. When I was cleaning his room yesterday he peeked around the corner, noticed I was working in semi-darkness, flipped on the light switch and said, "We have lights, too." Sweet guy.

I've never needed to read Rilke as much as I do out here. I'm memorizing my favorite part where he writes, "Resolve to be always beginning..." It has become my motto.

How is summer treating you? Do you have time in between classes to soak up a few rays and get a tan? My tan is on permanent leave.

I hope you're both doing well in school. I miss both of you so much. Take care.
Love,
Mom

I get up from my desk and get ready for bed. Then I remember something Rich told me earlier; we're supposed to set our clocks back before we go to sleep because we're entering the Alaska time zone tonight. "We get an extra hour of sleep," Rich said when I saw him in the passageway. "But we'll pay our dues on the trip south." I reset my two alarm clocks, turn out the light and crawl under the covers.

As I lie in the darkness, I listen to the rough seas. From outside comes the sound of metal on metal. Every time we hit a big swell, the ship reverberates as if in pain. It clangs once slowly, then twice quickly. C-l-a-n-g. Clang. Clang. From inside comes the even louder sound of my ricocheting heart. Even with my eyes closed I still see the giant wave crashing down on me.

N

W ⟵◇⟶ E

S

Chapter Six

Floating

The rough seas have quieted as the ship moves on. I'm outside on the deck when the sun rises over the snow-covered mountains in the Valdez passage. Pinks, apricots and magentas tint the Alaskan sky and waterfalls so exquisitely that I crumble to my knees. I don't know how long I kneel here on the cold steel absorbing the beauty. I only know that if I could save one sunrise to replay for the rest of my life, this would be the one.

Robby walks up behind me and takes a picture of the new day.

"It's beautiful, isn't it?" I say, looking up at him.

"The best," he responds.

A moment passes in silence. Then Robby says, "Hey. I was wondering, ah, Rich says you're a teacher."

"Yep. That's what I was doing before I got here. What is it you are wondering, Robby?"

"Could you maybe teach me how to read? I've struggled with dyslexia all my life, but I really want to learn."

I'm so touched by his openness, overwhelmed that he would ask me for help. I stand and look into his eyes. "Of course. I'd be honored. When would you like to start?"

While we discuss our tutoring session schedule, Robby points out two otters frolicking near the shore. Over and under the water they roll, dipping, sliding and jumping about in play. For a break, they lie on their backs, paws on their chests.

I don't want to leave this magical moment, but I know I must. It's time to get back to work. I say good-bye to Robby and reluctantly walk up the metal stairs to the galley with its abundant food smells. I walk in on Rich singing along with his oldies CD collection.

"Morning, Jeanne," he calls.

"Morning, Rich." Our standard routine. Rich brews hot water for his tea. I pull the mop bucket toward the officer's mess.

"How are you doing?" he asks.

"Rich, I'm so tired I couldn't even take a decent power nap yesterday. Kept waking myself up snoring."

"My wife says I snore even when I'm sleeping on my stomach. Didn't think that was humanly possible." He slaps his knee and hoots.

The galley phone rings. It's a call that spurs Rich into overdrive. Captain Figarino wants menus up on the bridge for himself and the Valdez pilot.

"Now leave the dishes and get ready to run," Rich says. "When you get up there, stand at the door, hand the menu to whoever greets you and don't speak until you're spoken to."

"Got it."

"Nobody's gonna bite you up there," Rich hollers as I dash out the galley door, menus in hand.

Fretting over ship protocol, I climb the four flights of stairs. The *dos* and *don'ts* of shipping make me nervous. I worry that I'm about to commit some major faux pas. I'm catching my breath outside the door to the bridge when Figarino greets me with a smile. Lips zipped, I hand him the menus and hang out in the doorway.

"You didn't take the elevator up here?" he asks.

"No sir," I say.

"I'm teasing you. The elevator doesn't go past D Deck." He chuckles and turns away.

In the middle of the room, an AB stands at the helm taking course directions from the Alaskan pilot. The instruments and gauges make my mouth water; I'd love to learn navigation. Maybe one day I will tell the captain. It's all windows up here in the bridge. Windows, gauges and charts spread out on a big drafting table. A 360 degree view shows off the Valdez countryside, pristine except for the gigantic oil terminal across the bay from town.

After he orders for himself and the pilot, the captain surprises me. "Jeanne, do you have a camera?" he asks.

"Yes, sir. In my room."

"Bring it up after breakfast and take some pictures of this lovely scenery."

"Great. Thanks, sir."

"Come over here, Jeanne. I want to show you something," he says and motions me to a side door that leads outside to the bridge wing. "It's not like you're trapped down on B Deck. This is a nice spot. Visit whenever you want."

"And don't bother with my room today," he adds. "Too much stuff happening in port."

I feel like singing! Feel like slapping him on the back and telling him a good story. Feel like doing my yippee, good-times-are-here dance. Instead I calmly say, "Thanks, sir."

I dash down to Rich in the galley and place the captain's order. I prepare myself for the morning rush, then run breakfast up the stairs for Figarino and the pilot. He smiles at me and reminds me about the pictures.

The dishes seem to clean themselves this morning. All I can think about is getting up to the bridge for fifteen precious minutes to take the photos I'll show to everyone back home. Photos of snow-covered mountains reaching down to pristine blue water fill my head. I cannot wait to take these pictures. I don't even notice the burning steam of the third step to cleaning the dishes. In my mind I am already on the bridge.

On my break I run to my room, grab my camera and scurry up the stairs that lead to the bridge. I am anxious to take the first shot—as if all of this natural, serene beauty will disappear before I can focus the camera. I quickly scan the shoreline and snap several shots of the mountains and of the waves crashing on the shore. I try to take a picture of everything from the glaciers to the forest to the town and back again. I even take a photo of some of the gadgets on the bridge.

When I finish, I thank the captain once again and go back to my room. The excitement of getting to take those photos gave me extra energy after my morning tasks, but now I'm tired. In the few spare moments I have before I go back to my duties, I write a letter to my daughters.

At sea outside Valdez, Alaska
Dear Emily and Lisa,

Today Robby told me that he'd gone through the public school system without knowing he had dyslexia, so he never understood why it was so hard for him to learn how to read. While watching the Valdez sunrise, he leaned over and whispered, "Jeanne, will you teach me to read?"

I'm always blown away by the courage it takes for an adult to ask that question. I stood there in complete awe of his bravery and vulnerability. All I could do was nod and tell him it would be my pleasure.

He told me about school and how reading was always impossible. He tried hard but never got it. His childhood in Honolulu was nothing short of miraculous. He survived gun shot wounds, knifings, unfounded arrests. For the past fifteen years he's worked non-stop on ships to support his mother and two sisters. I've always seen Robby as a strong and amazing person, but now he seems even more incredible to me.

He didn't know he was dyslexic until a few years ago. He reached for his wallet and took out a piece of paper the size of an ID card on which a psychologist's diagnosis was written : severe dyslexia and ADHD. He told me he carries this card everywhere now, so people know to give him extra time to fill out forms and stuff.

I asked him what he'd most like to read if he could. Without hesitation he told me, "I really wanted to become a chief cook but couldn't pass the written tests. I didn't know that I qualified for a verbal exam." I told him that we would start working on that goal tomorrow.

"Soon you'll be reading Rich's cook books," I promised him. I plan on asking Rich what kinds of questions are on the test so Robby will know how to study. We agreed to meet twice a week during the first half-hour of my break.

If I were lying on my deathbed, Robby's smile, like both of yours, would be a good thing to see. I guess once a teacher, always a teacher, eh?
All my love,
Mom

P.S. As soon as I get my film developed I'll send a few pictures of Valdez. It's breathtaking out here with the snow-capped mountains towering above lush forests and a beautiful rocky coast. You have to see it to believe it. When I first laid eyes on it, the emotions I felt were so powerful I was reminded of the days I gave birth to each of you. Have I ever told you about that? My grandma had always told me that children are on loan from God, and she was right. When the nurse handed each of you to me, all brand new, naked and shiny, you both looked like underwater starbursts placed in my arms. Truly amazing!

This afternoon as I enter the galley, it's filled with the smell of melted chocolate. Rich is baking his delicious chocolate chip, peanut butter and oatmeal raisin cookies on baking sheets each the size of half a door. They're the ready-made, prefab kind Rich started baking when the Valdez alcohol regulations tightened up. The cookies give the crew something to look forward to in a port where drinking is strictly prohibited. With oven mitts on his big hands, Rich lifts an orderly beauty of melted chips and warm dough out of the oven. I'm pouring a glass of milk when Rich starts up.

"Yep. Go ashore here and pay the price," Rich says. "Taxi search. Body frisk. Breathalyzer. When a mariner goes to shore in Valdez, he's scrutinized before he gets back on board. At the terminal's main gate his taxi is searched for alcohol while he goes inside, shows his Z card, walks through a scanner, gets hand-frisked and then, if he's acting a little strangely, he's given a breathalyzer test. Ever since the big spill, one beer is enough to end a shipping career."

"Is this town any fun?" I ask.

"There's plenty of girl stuff. Shops filled with little doodads. They even got them lattes." He pronounces lattes, lay-tays.

"Well, I'm going to investigate."

"Bring me back a newspaper, would ya?" Rich asks. "Any newspaper with any date on it."

I run back to my room to change out of my grubby clothes. I put on clean, black jeans and a fresh shirt. Heading out for town, I whistle as I climb the movable stairs that lead from the ship to the dock. I'm halfway across the bridge over the small bay when I notice Chief Engineer Scruggs walking back toward the ship.

"Road's closed. Some fucking crane tipped over. It's blocking traffic in both directions. It won't be fixed before tomorrow," he says disgustedly.

"We can't even get into town?" I ask. "There must be some way."

"No goddamned way. It's the road or nothing. No launches here."

Side-by-side, we trudge back toward the ship. Finally, Scruggs breaks the silence when he asks, "Hey, what were you doing before you started shipping?"

"I was a part-time English instructor at a college."

He looks at me like I'm sprouting wings. "No shit. What in the hell are you doing here?"

"Trying to make financial ends meet."

I give him the college instructor speech, the one about how seventy-five percent of all college instructors are now adjunct, part-time, paid a pittance per class. How only twenty-five percent of those teaching are full-time and paid an annual salary with benefits.

"I had the best case scenario for a part-timer at a great university, and even then I was only bringing home around $1200 a month," I say.

He looks across the bay toward town shaking his head. We both stay silent for the remainder of our walk.

Later, Rich jumps like he's seeing an apparition when I come down in the mid-afternoon to set up for dinner. I relay the news of the blocked road, my plan to try again after dinner.

"No launches. Road's closed," he says matter-of-factly. "Better face it. You're in for the night."

"But I still have your permission, right? And the captain still knows you've given me shore privileges?"

"Oh yeah, yeah," he says, but I can almost see his thoughts written in the air, *You're never gonna make it.*

After dinner, on my way to the big stair contraption that goes up and over the ship, Robby and Stanley heckle me. "Where ya going Jeanne? Road's closed. We're all prisoners tonight."

"I'm going to town."

I walk across the bridge connecting the O.S. Illinois to land. I enter the port building, which is the closest building to our ship, and find a clerk inside.

"What can I do for you?" the young man asks.

"I am trying to get into town, but the road is closed. Is there any way I can hitch a ride on someone's boat?"

He thinks for a moment, looks me in the eyes and dials a number. Someone picks up the other line. "What time's the SERV boat taking the Terminal workers across to town? Yeah. Yep. Got a crew member here on Berth 4 who wants to catch it. Pick her up by the phones?"

"It must be your lucky day," he smiles at me and says. "A shift at the Terminal just ended and we've got a big SERV ferry taking the workers across the harbor. Road closed or not, people need to get home."

He explains that SERV is an organization that started up after the Valdez spill. Now they've got boats, a big headquarters and a variety of environmental jobs.

"Just walk across the bridge to the phones and wait for a red pickup. Don't walk down the road to the harbor. Too many bears."

My lucky day. Though I love the sea I'm becoming more convinced that I am a land lover at heart. Once or twice I skip and jump, then I walk across the steady, non-moving bridge. The further I get from the ship, the better I feel. I'm a real woman again, smelling good, hair down, out on the town. For this one sweet night, I'm free as a bird. Let them do their own dishes! The red pickup takes me down to the small harbor where I'm whisked onto the SERV ferry filled with tired, sweaty workers. In my pocket is tucked the SERV twenty-four-hour phone number for the ride back.

I watch the O.S. Illinois grow smaller on the far side of the harbor as the SERV ferry pulls into the town of Valdez. There are so many sights to see. Women push babies in strollers. Two teenage boys with blaring headsets dance past. An elderly gentleman sweeps the front steps of his shop. So much to see and hear. So much to choose from. So much freedom.

I admire the Alaskan landscape, which is full of near and distant greens, snow-covered mountains, a clear powder-blue sky and sparkling water. The smell of snow fills the air even though it's summer. The sound of small boats bobbing past us in the harbor lingers in my ears. I reflect on the smallness of man against the splendor and vastness of Alaska stretching up and outward forever. Enthralled with the wonder of it, I walk on land, notice every bird, every sound, every reminder of the joys of being earth bound.

The first place I stop when I get to dry land is the Visitor's Bureau where I pick up a map. It tells me that there are only two main streets in Valdez. This is a good thing because I have only three objectives I must accomplish quickly in Valdez. First, I wanted to get here, because everyone said it was impossible. One down, two to go. Second, I need to buy a newspaper for Rich and a large chocolate bar for myself at a grocery store. That should be no problem. Finally, I want to phone my oldest daughter in California. I wish I could call Lisa, but it's too late to call Michigan from this time zone.

I find the closest convenient store on the map, Eagle Grocery Store, and head for it. I pick up a newspaper for Rich and a large Cadbury chocolate bar for myself. Outside the store I rip open the candy bar wrapper, bite off a chunk of the dark chocolate and head to the pay phone in the corner of the parking lot. I call Emily hoping that she answers. She picks up on the second ring.

"Hi honey, it's Mom," I say.

"Mom! How are you? I've been so worried about you. It's so good to hear your voice." Her voice cracks as she finishes her sentence. My eyes begin to water. I'm already crying just when I hear her begin to sob.

"I know it's silly Mom, but I've missed you more just knowing there was no way to reach you."

"I know, honey. I feel the same way."

For half-an-hour we talk. People walk by me as I sit here eating my chocolate bar, crying, laughing and relating my experiences to Emily.

"Are you safe, Mom? Are the guys gentlemen?"

"Yes, yes," I promise her, "gentle across the board." I don't mention Marty's crass pick-up lines or Al's nasty attitude.

It's far better than the chocolate bar when I say to Emily, "I love you. I miss you." She repeats the words to me and I'm connected again to something greater than myself.

I'm tired and sleepy when we hang up. It's already 9:30 P.M., so I walk toward the harbor, amazed that it's still light outside at this hour. My heart fills with longing for my daughters and friends, and I'm so tired that my legs and feet inch along. If I had one wish at this very moment, it would be that I could sleep in the best hotel room in Valdez on crisp, clean sheets that have never been touched by anything so crude as a mariner's mattress. I would sleep until noon tomorrow, later if necessary. Then I'd order room service. Strong French roast coffee, extra hot and laced with fresh cream, Eggs Benedict, a croissant with real butter and raspberry jam and fresh strawberries. I'd eat it all in bed on exquisite English china at my leisure while I read fashion magazines, the kind where looking at the photos of the newest styles is more important than the text. I wouldn't want to get too involved in a story which might interest me so much that I wouldn't be able to turn over and go back to sleep until three in the afternoon, at which time I'd take a slow, steaming bubble bath. I'd listen to classical violin music interspersed with an occasional Pavarotti aria and Bob Dylan tune while I cleansed my body of the filth it has picked up from my work on the ship. Dinner, of course, would be the freshest seafood and salad with the best Italian red wine, followed by strawberries dipped in the world's finest chocolate. In reality, my finger touches the SERV number in my pocket. I should be getting back to the ship now that I have completed all of my objectives. There is a man walking toward me who looks very familiar. It takes me a moment, but I realize that he greeted people on the ferry. Turns out his name is John and his buddy, Tony, works at SERV headquarters. He gives Tony a call on his cell phone and tells him to pick us up.

As we wait for our ride, John distracts me by telling me the story about how he came to Alaska. "It was a dream of mine for a long, long time. I used to tell everyone that I was going to move up here, but I never took any action until my brother started yelling at me one day when I was dreaming out loud. 'I'm sick and tired of hearing you talk and talk about Alaska. Why don't you just ante up and do it?' Well, that hit me right between the eyes, and here I am. Been here for twenty years with my wife and we love it."

No sooner does John finish his story than Tony arrives in his rig to drive us to the SERV headquarters. Upon

learning that I am from the O.S. Illinois, Tony mentions,
"Your captain is in town too. You'll be riding back with him
as soon as he finishes dinner."

At headquarters they check my Z card, but no frisk-
ing, no breathalyzer. I act nonchalant while Tony gives me
the tour of their offices. Normally, I'd be impressed, but I'm
exhausted and all I can think about is sitting down. When
the tour is over, I go to the chairs and curl up in one. Though
the chair is made of hard, uncomfortable plastic, I find a way
to contort my body so that I can rest somewhat comfortably
and take a nap. I fade away quickly, sleep for a few minutes
and awake just in time to see Captain Figarino walk through
the big security doors.

He does a double-take when he sees me.

"I didn't know another seaman from the Illinois
made it across," he says to Tony while glancing over at me.
Figarino straightens his collar, smoothes down his shirt, runs
his palms against the sides of his hair, then sits down beside
me.

"You don't waste any time, do you? Do you have any
idea how long it takes most people to get a ride on a SERV
boat, if ever?"

"No, sir," I respond. "I don't know how long it usually
takes most people. And no, sir. I don't waste time."

He stares at me and shakes his head in disbelief.

I wonder how to explain to a linear thinker the curi-
ous life and serendipitous happenings of a circular thinker

who's lead by intuition and the belief that things usually work out. "Nothing is impossible" is a credo I've believed in for a long time.

Figarino looks a little disheveled and I speculate as to whether the rumor about him having an affair is true, and if so, what his mistress looks like.

We make our way to a small, half-covered, gunmetal boat. The captain and I ride across the harbor. There the red pickup waits to drive us back to our ship. When we get to the truck, we see it is a two-seater, so we will have to ride back to the ship separately. Figarino extends his arm toward the red door and slightly, ever so slightly, lowers his head.

"Jeanne. You first. I insist."

The drive on the gravel road sends me nodding off, only to half wake up at the port building next to the ship. Sleepily I begin to climb the metal stairs, which seem significantly lower now. I climb up and across but stop abruptly when I see a smooth, freshly painted gray deck. My mind knows something is wrong, and I awaken from my daze. The Illinois deck is chipped and rusted green. This is not my ship! I immediately turn to walk off the ship when I hear a voice.

"Hey sweet thing. Want to sail with the California?" calls an AB from the deck below.

"Afraid I can't. I'm attached to another ship," I say. I can't help smiling. "I have rooms to clean in the morning."

"We got rooms. Sail with us."

I run back across and down the stairs to the port building and tell the guy on watch what happened. "The driver took you to Berth 5 instead of Berth 4." He stifles a laugh and calls the pickup guy, who shows up within minutes, busting his gut laughing.

Robby waits for me at the bottom of the stairs on the Illinois. "Thinking about sailing on the California?" he asks.

"Maybe," I say.

"How long before you knew it was the wrong ship?"

"Long enough to almost get a date." We both chuckle.

"You got lots of mail." He pats my shoulder. "I put it in front of the door to your room."

Tired but content, I climb the stairs to my room, lie down on the bunk and read the mail I received from home. My oldest daughter asks what I need in a care package. A colleague sends her summer reading list and a letter stating her disbelief that I'm working on an oil tanker, of all things. An aunt writes about the passing of my uncle and encloses the memorial service card. I remember him being a shy, kind soul. His death makes me think about my ill father. I fall asleep with the light on, letters and envelopes on top of the blankets next to me.

I awake the next morning in the same position with the letters and envelopes all heaped around me. Sitting on the edge of my bunk, hands so swollen I can barely tie my boots, I gather my strength for another long day of work. I soak my hands in warm water before I can brush my teeth and get dressed. I've told Robby and Rich about the swelling. Robby thinks it's sore muscles. Rich thinks that the harsh cleaning chemicals seep through the rubber gloves and cause it. He's known other steward assistants who've had this happen. I think squeezing the tongs to lift the heavy plates, pots and pans out of the scalding water is what's doing it.

At breakfast Robby approaches me looking like a Tai Chi instructor. He moves gracefully, his arms and legs synchronized, so lithe that even in his steel-toed boots he draws near in silence. He looks like he's bursting to tell his favorite joke as he hands me a tube of BenGay. "Hope this helps your hands. I have an extra. Keep it," he says.

He turns to leave before I have time to say more than, "Thanks." I watch him walk down the passageway, a radiant, winged-being in orange coveralls. I wonder what's got him in such a grand mood.

We disembark from Valdez port early that morning. We leave well within the standard twenty-four-hour turn-around time. In the mess hall I glance out the porthole at Valdez and can't help but think that we won't see land for a week. I'm back in my other life. At sea it's only the water, the sky and the hum of the engine. It's repetition of days passing quickly, one after the other. It's the same old routine of meals and drills, meals and rooms. It's dishes rattling, knives chopping vegetables and Rich saying, "Umhumh. Yeah." Then again, it is also the time that you get to see the most gorgeous sunsets and stars.

Dinner runs its normal course and afterward Rich teases me, "You know, once I've finished reading that newspaper you bought me, I'll just have to start in on your mail since you're the only one who got any."

When I mention that one of the letters informed me of my uncle's passing, Rich says, "Sorry to hear that," and politely leaves me alone at the sink.

During my morning cleaning duties, I stop working in Scrugg's bathroom for a moment to cry at the smell of Lava soap. The engineers use this soap to cut the grease on their hands. When I clean the sink, I rinse off the bar so that it doesn't sit there all scummy on the clean, white porcelain. And now, unbidden, come memories of Grandma, hand-washing knees of grass-stained jeans, Grandpa washing up for dinner and me using the soap because I wanted to be just like them.

I rinse the bar of soap one last time, inhale its fragrance and remember my grandma's house full of the love and care she always gave me. And now here I am, hundreds of miles out at sea, mothering the men whose rooms I clean and dishes I scrub. I sigh. Once a mother, always a mother.

But sometimes, I think as I look into the bathroom mirror, *the crew mothers me right back.*

After finishing the bathroom I plunge deep into my other morning chores, feeling oddly sad and happy at the same time with the memory of my grandparents tucked away near my heart.

The next room down the hall is Chuck's. I must say I'm pleasantly surprised by some of the men out here, men like Chuck. He is the oldest QMED on the ship and will disembark for his vacation when we arrive at Long Beach, California. His four months are up and he's ready to get home to his wife in Alabama. On the door to his room hangs a calendar with his days crossed off. Only three to go. The picture above these dates is of a red barn surrounded by green grass and tall oak trees. It reminds me of the farm where I grew up.

Chuck is only a few months younger than Stanley, has tattoos up and down each arm and always wears black pants and a T-shirt when he comes down for dinner. A sweet gentleman, his southern accent reminds me of the smell of magnolias and the feel of the heat on a warm summer afternoon. Every now and then when I look at him in the mess hall, I see what he must have looked like at eighteen: thin body, thick black hair, same twinkling blue eyes. He always has a smile and a kind word. At lunch he asks about my daughters, what they do for a living. "I hope they'll have better paying jobs than teaching adjunct classes like their mom," he says softly.

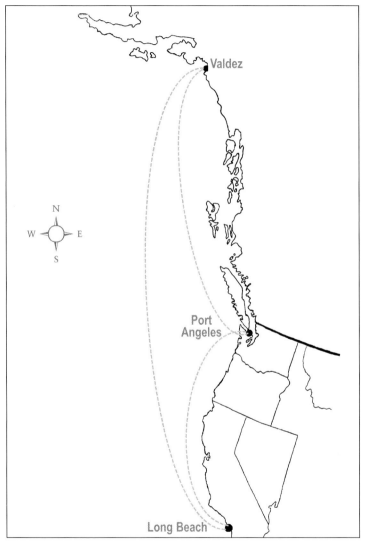

This map shows the route and major ports the O.S. Illinois traveled to while Jeanne Lutz was a crewmember: Long Beach, California, Port Angeles, Washington and Valdez, Alaska.

The O.S. Illinois at sea, looking from bow to stern. When Jeanne boards the ship, she longs for adventure but wonders if she has made the right decision.

Jeanne often walks the decks of the O.S. Illinois at sunset contemplating her future.

The stunning natural beauty of the straits of Valdez, Alaska, is evident in this aerial view.

As the ship enters the straits of Valdez, the captain invites Jeanne to shoot photos from the bridge.

The bridge railings frame the majestic mountains lining the straits of Valdez.

Wearing her Steward Assistant uniform—khaki pants and white shirt—Jeanne takes a break to enjoy the view.

The O.S. Illinois sails into Valdez Harbor to pick up its freight—oil.

Though off duty, Jeanne and all crewmembers are required to wear hardhats on deck when the ship is in port.

Letters, pictures and care packages from her two daughters, Lisa and Emily, sustain Jeanne through some of the toughest times on the ship.

Through her experiences as a merchant marine, Jeanne Lutz makes peace with her past and finds strength in herself.

I nod, "They definitely will."

Ray sits at the table next to us. He's another favorite of mine. I perk up a little when I hear him order his favorite breakfast for lunch before he sits down. "Three eggs over easy with grits, sausage and a short stack," he says. Ray is back. He's a jovial, strong, black AB from Alabama who can put away groceries like nobody's business. Sadly, however, for the past few days he's been trying to lose weight by eating mostly rice.

"Pot roast with potatoes and gravy, Ray?" Rich asked yesterday at lunch.

"No sir. Rice. Rice and a few of those green beans there," Ray laughed, but his laughter wasn't as strong and deep as it usually is. His smile wasn't quite as broad as usual, either.

While on this diet he caught me slathering chocolate sauce over my chocolate chip cookie dough ice cream in the crew mess after lunch.

"How come you can eat that and stay so skinny?" he asked.

"I don't know, Ray. Life is short. I'd eat it even if I were chubby. I like it."

"There you go. You go girl," was all he said.

There are no more worries. It appears his diet is over. His laughter and grin affirm Ray's return. Apparently he is going to have a few nice meals before he disembarks in Long Beach.

After breakfast I walk up to the bridge for some last pictures of Valdez. Camera in hand, I'm greeted by the Alaskan pilot who comes outside to talk with me. He gets so carried away telling me about Alaska that the ship veers port side straight toward a mountain. We're so close to the edge of the channel that the captain comes outside to get him.

"We need a course adjustment," Figarino hollers.

"Excuse me," the pilot says. "I should be changing course." As he runs inside his words echo in my mind.

Rich is standing on the starboard bridge wing looking through binoculars, as all this occurs. I walk over to see if he'll take my picture. As usual, he's talking to himself but snaps a photo of me in my orange hard hat with the Alaskan mountains and Valdez Channel at my back.

Later, while we are cleaning the galley together, he asks me if I thought he was talking to himself up on the bridge today. I'm not sure why he is asking this or what kind of answer he expects. "Yeah, I thought you were looking through binoculars and talking to yourself just as you usually do in the galley."

He laughs and replies, "I was talking to my wife with my cell earphones on. I didn't want you to think I was ignoring you or being rude." I chuckle when I hear that. And all this time I thought he was a nice guy, but a bit off his rocker for talking to himself! As we continue our duties he talks about dancing with his wife Carmen.

"Lord, I have to drink a keg and a half of beer just so I look like I know what I'm doing when I go salsa dancing with her. I always spend the next day resting my knees cause they get all knocked around."

Rich must sense my melancholy mood. He bakes a devil's food cake for dessert and begins joking with me. "You know, that piece of cake has your name written all over it. You will have to eat it or take it with you 'cause my room's right across the hall from yours, and I don't want to hear that cake calling you in the middle of the night." He smiles and winks at me as we finish wiping the tables down.

I'm touched by the little things some of the tough mariners do out here. Rich lifting my spirits and making sure I eat good food, Robby giving helpful gifts. Tender sailors. Their kindness reminds me of one of my rare good memories of my father. It was the day he took me for swimming lessons after I'd almost drowned.

Before the afternoon milking, Dad drove me to the town pool and asked me to show him where I was when I'd jumped in. He jumped in right there, in the exact same spot, held out his arms to me and told me to jump, that he'd catch me. I looked into his eyes for a second, then jumped. The cool water splashed on my feet and legs but never came close to my head. He put me up on his

shoulders and began walking toward the deep end. First
the water hit his waist, then his shoulders, then his chin.
I started to get afraid, but Dad showed another part of
himself to me that day. He did something that lessened
my fear of drowning. He slowly lowered his head under
the water until only I was high above, breathing air. He
surfaced and went under, surfaced and went under, and
I experienced a feeling of floating. I was near the deep
end, safe and floating, victor over the water. Victor over
him, too.

The next week when I started swimming lessons, I
was the only kid to pass the first section on the first day:
floating.

Tenderness in a very dark heart. I think of my bittersweet past then devour that delicious slice of cake. I make my
way back to my room. I'm tired, but I've been meaning to
write to the friend who helped me get started in this crazy
new career.

Dear Cheryl,

   I've started several letters but for one reason or another,
I've thrown them all away. Too much to catch up on and never
enough time to say it right. However, before I begin the summary

version, I want to say how much I miss you and wish that you were on this ship with me. I hope your job is going well, you're finding time "just for you" to relax and you're having a little fun.

I moved to Portland at the end of June. While I got settled in the new house, I met great, absolutely wonderful neighbors who insisted on checking my mail and mowing my yard while I was at sea. The community I live in is very friendly and close-knit.

I sat for three weeks in the Seafarer's International Union Hall waiting for an assignment. During this time I met several sailors and got to know the lingo of shipping. I also had some more time to reflect upon myself and where I am going in life.

Finally, a sixty day relief job came up on the board on the O.S. Illinois. A B-Card threw in for it, but didn't have his drug test. Fred York, an official at the union, made a big deal out of it and gave him the night to get things straightened away.

When I showed up on the second day, the guy still didn't have the information on his drug test, so I heard, "Jeanne! Get up here and bring your stuff. You've got an assignment."

Fred, he's quite a character. I can't help but like him even though his parting remark after I signed up was, "You're gonna work your ass off."

So, on July 24, I arrived in Port Angeles, Washington and boarded the O.S. Illinois, an oil tanker. Fred was right about working my tail off, because the guy I replaced hadn't done diddly-squat except for cleaning the captain's and chief engineer's rooms; the other eight rooms were a disgusting disaster. Did I mention that the dishwasher was broken? Oh, it still is. I wash all the dishes, pots and pans by hand—for the entire crews' three meals each day.

My chief steward is a great boss. He's a good family man who cracks corny jokes and is very kind to me. He tells me the trade secrets about cleaning the showers with floor stripper and how to pull the bedding all the way under the mattress "to keep them boys from going anywhere in their sleep." He's a peach.

Different members of the crew have been complimenting me on my cleaning. Despite the compliments, it's a nightmare of a job. I have to clean everything in ten rooms: sinks, toilets, showers and floors.

The captain is a well-built man with a strong presence about him. I feel like I'm always doing dumb stuff around him because he makes me nervous, but he seems to find it amusing. Still, for the most part, he's been very kind to me and has gone out of his way to be helpful and appreciative.

A couple of guys have acted a little "dopey" around me since I'm the only woman on board. There are a few really attractive ones, but none are my type. Heck, I don't even know what my type is at this point. Probably a good thing too, after Fred York gave me a sex lecture shortly before I got the assignment.

Did I say where the ship goes? We pick up cargo—oil—in Valdez, Alaska, and take it to either Los Angeles, San

Francisco or a port city in Washington. Right now we're leaving Valdez and heading for Los Angeles.

I haven't been sleeping well due to pain and numbness in my hands. When I awake in the morning, my fingers are so swollen that I can barely move them. I know that it's from chemicals and the lack of a dishwasher. I am praying that the gods will give me some insight into how to heal. I did my yoga for the first time on board and I felt better. Maybe if I continue with it, my hands will improve. Only time will tell...

Every once in a while there is some tension on the ship between certain members of the crew, but for the most part we are all friendly. I do my best to get along with everyone and I feel that most of them appreciate my friendliness. They all seem to want to tell me their shipping stories.

Anais Nin says that writers lead a double life: the one they live, then the one they relive as they write it, process it, rediscover it anew. I think she's right not only about writers but all of us.

I am growing weary so before I take my leave I want to thank you once again for informing me that women can be in the merchant marines. I am now living my dream because you told me that I could work in shipping. Thank you.

Love,

Jeanne

After I seal the envelope, I'm truly exhausted. I'm barely able to pull the covers over me before I fall into a deep sleep. The days are passing by, but they are bringing me to new levels of fatigue. I've never felt this way before. I'm tired when I fall asleep, tired when I wake. It seems like I am a walking zombie some days. I sleep like a rock most nights.

When I start my rounds in the morning I'm still groggy, but awake enough to overhear one of the guy's in the captain's office cussing like a sailor. Then I see Figarino standing in the doorway and hear him call someone an asshole. I clean two more rooms and as I walk past the captain's office, he calls out my name. I back up and stand in front of his room. He has a sheepish look on his face.

"Jeanne, I apologize for the crude language the men use from time to time on the ship. I know it isn't proper, and I'm sorry that a lady has to hear such language. I only use it at sea, never around my wife or mother."

"No problem, sir," I reassure him. "I use it myself, from time to time."

"Well again, I'm sorry."

"Apology accepted, sir."

Once upon a time when our ship, the O.S. Illinois, was young, there was a room next to mine with a shared bathroom in between. Now that room serves as a large linen storage closet. Except for the large wooden shelves where the bed used to be, the linen closet is no different from my room. I'm in the closet before dinner, wildly making piles of items of useless junk: an assortment of broken fans, a vacuum cleaner that doesn't work, used shower curtains, stained sheets and towels that I handle only with rubber gloves. I throw five empty cardboard boxes into the passageway, scrunch crummy stuff into two large plastic trash bags until they stand chest high, then spot six open cases of strawberry air freshener, a symbol of the lazy slob who left me so much work. Apparently Marty's understanding of cleaning a room was walking in and spraying air freshener everywhere. Tearing into one of the boxes of *Sweet Breeze*, I arrange the cans on a shelf.

My temper flares. "Marty, you lazy piece of unmitigated horse shit!"

The words hang vibrant in the air when I notice someone standing in the passageway eyeing the strewn boxes. It's Figarino.

I have the distinct impression he's happy, delighted actually, to hear me cuss. He looks from the boxes to me, drenched with sweat and hopping mad.

"Sir, it's a mess in here." I push the fallen hair off my face, shift my weight to one leg.

"I see," he says, grinning big. "Jeanne, I know you're busy, but I need you to make up the spare room on D Deck for the new third engineer getting on in Long Beach. He'll overlap one night with the guy he's replacing."

"Right away, sir."

"Thank you," he says, stepping carefully around the boxes. "Unmitigated horse shit. That's a good one," he mumbles on his way out.

At dinner the message board outside the crew mess reads, "Draw Bridge/2200." I translate that to mean we go under a drawbridge on our way into Long Beach at 10:00 P.M.

"What does the drawbridge look like?" I ask Rich while doing dishes.

"Is it cool? I mean, is it worth staying up late to see?"

His face gets all contorted, he tries not to grin, but he can't help himself. He bends over, slaps his knee three times, stomps his foot and comes up laughing so hard he's practically choking on his own breath.

"There's no drawbridge, Jeanne. At ten tonight there's a draw on the bridge. You take a draw on your pay." He laughs some more. "Can't let this one slide. I'm gonna have to tell the captain this one."

As I take my evening stroll on the deck, Rich walks toward me wearing a hooded sweatshirt tied tightly around his red face. I am bare-headed, hair flying in the refreshing breeze. We meet at the bow in time to see a pod of porpoises riding the bow wave in front of the ship. Despite the rumor that this happens regularly, it's the first time I have seen it. They are sleek and gray. Their faces look as though they're smiling up at us. I talk with them. Rich stares at me as if I've lost my wits, but I don't care.

"I've never seen so many," he says. "I figure there must be at least a hundred."

The porpoises love to surf. Rich says you can see them playing around big ships every once in a while. We stand on the bow and watch as they catch the curl. Then I notice that they're accompanied by brown, velvet-skinned seals that race and frolic alongside them. I wish I could glide effortlessly through the waters as they do.

Rich returns to the house as I gaze out at the sea, empty now that the porpoises have left. It's a clear evening, one that casts a spell upon the gray water, turning it myriad shades of blue. Tonight the horizon line beckons bright with sunlight. Tonight everything seems possible. Tonight I will stay out on deck as long as I can before I head up to my room for sleep. I want to see the stars. I walk up the stairs to the topmost part of the bow above where it's quiet, away from engine noise. It is the only place on the ship where I can be alone outside without being seen by anyone. I sit behind a big white box that holds extra lines. I squeeze into just the right spot behind it, so no one can see me from anywhere on the ship, not even the bridge. But I can still see the star-strewn sky above and can even glimpse the undulating waves below through the round anchor chain hole.

Before I go inside, I stand very still and lean over the bow railing, looking down at the deep indigo water, tinged with cerulean blue and white. I make a small circle with my thumb and index finger and look through it at the sea rushing beneath my makeshift porthole. The water changes from whitest white to dark blue to cotton-candy blue, over and over.

N

W ←⊕→ E

S

Chapter Seven

Long Beach Adventure

During the night we arrive in Long Beach, California. Mariners call this port El Segundo. The ship is not attached to the dock, but rather anchored out in the harbor on the hook. When we want to go ashore from this secondary dock, a launch will have to come out to the O.S. Illinois, pick us up and take us to the main dock.

Before sunrise, I take a quick walk outside and glance around. I think I see men in black diving gear. Fifty or more surround the ship in little white boats. "Maybe they are connecting oil pipes under the ship." I murmur as I try to figure out what they could possibly be doing. A moment later I hear a bark. One of the divers moves like a seal. Instantly, I realize my error—they are all seals! The creatures lie side-by-side like sardines in an open can, nine or ten stretched across each white buoy, heads hanging off one side, back flippers off the other. I move closer to the end of the deck and as my eyes adjust, I see some are black, some are reddish-brown and the big ones are covered with crusted barnacles unlike other seals I've seen. No circus tricks for these guys.

Just as the first rays of sun peek out from under the horizon, I see the reason we are at this port. In the distance to the left of our ship are large vertical and horizontal pipes, trucks and storage tanks. Oil. Straight ahead and to the right of our ship lies the city of Long Beach and it's environs. Gentle rolling hills and buildings provide a welcome break from the accustomed flat horizon line of the sea. I feel excitement in my chest at the sight and smell of land with its real people living real lives: families, lovers, schools, dirt, gardens, banks and businesses. Soon the rising sun sheds light over Long Beach. Distant hills, skyscrapers, boats, even the oil rigs look like a painting. I rush off to clean the rooms and help with breakfast.

Chief Engineer Scruggs comes through the breakfast chow line feeling chatty. "What's up with the rumor that we have a new QMED coming aboard whose name is Vanessa?"

Everyone laughs but me.

"Makes no difference to me that a QMED is female unless she's doesn't like my food," Rich says. His version of politically correct.

There is some banter on the subject through breakfast, but for the most part nothing is said about the new QMED until Scruggs returns to the chow line at lunch. This time he is complaining about how the female QMED called from the airport earlier in the day. "I don't have enough money for a taxi. Somebody come and get me," he mimics in an annoying, high-pitched voice.

I know she can't be a QMED (qualified man in the engine department) unless she's had prior experience in the engine room as a wiper. So unlike Scruggs, I don't mock her. She must have experience. She has to know what she is doing. Yet I do wonder why she's out of money. Maybe she's a single parent. Maybe she's in the middle of a divorce. Maybe she has large medical bills. Regardless of who she is and what she may be going through, I'm looking forward to meeting Vanessa. It will be great having another woman on board.

I do not have to wait long. As I head out the big steel door on my afternoon walk, I collide with a woman. My first impression of her is that she reminds me of Annie Oakley in *Annie Get Your Gun*. She's short, feisty and cute. Her friendly face features dark brown eyes set wide apart, a button nose and a full mouth. By the looks of her arms, she either lifts weights or has a physically demanding job.

"Oh my God! The first person I see on this ship is another woman. Can I say how glad I am to meet you?" she says in a southern drawl.

"Hi, I'm Jeanne."

"Vanessa, the new QMED." She takes my hand in both of hers and shakes it enthusiastically.

"What do you do on the ship, Jeanne?"

"S.A. This is my first ship," I reply.

"Oh, you poor kid."

We walk the deck together, talking, two women on a steel ship surrounded by men.

"This is my fifth ship, but my first one alone. I usually ship with my boyfriend," she says.

"Where is he?" I ask her.

"Back home in Texas waiting for an assignment." She stops and looks up at me. "I'm gonna tell you, because I feel like you're a good person." She laughs a bit nervously. "I took this sixty-day relief job to get away from him. He's got a temper, ya know?"

I nod.

"After our last big argument, I got really scared." She doesn't say anymore, but I see the wounded look in her eyes.

"How did you get started in the engine room?" I ask to redirect the conversation.

"Jed, my boyfriend, he got me into shipping. Said it was good money and I was smart enough to be a QMED."

"So you're comfortable down there with all those machines."

She turns to me. "That's just it. This ancient piece-of-shit ship is a steam. I've only worked on diesels before."

"It's a big difference?"

"Nothing's the same. Plus, with steam, there are all the valves. Everything's big and heavy. But I got muscles, right?" She rolls up her T-shirt sleeve and flexes her bulging biceps.

I try to be sympathetic, but having no knowledge of what it's like to work in the engine room, I feel my words of encouragement must sound hollow. Trying to be helpful I show Vanessa to her room and leave her to finish my chores as she unpacks.

I'm too tired to go ashore tonight. Some of the crew are catching the eight o'clock launch, but if I join them, the earliest I can get back to the ship is just before midnight. I'm too exhausted go out, get back that late and get up at 4:30 for work tomorrow morning. I decide to wait until tomorrow afternoon to go ashore when I can linger, go shopping, and call my kids and friends.

After dinner, I walk the deck to the topmost part of the bow, where I'm surrounded by white-gray seagulls. Spreading their wings, they caw, swooping down over the lines. Seals bark from the buoys. I stay until the strong wind makes me so cold my hands turn blue and icy, then I head to a spot that's more sheltered. I gaze at the colored sunset smog and listen to the sounds of land: traffic, honking cars, trains, sirens, airplanes overhead. Tonight, in my fatigue, I take in the sounds I didn't realize I'd missed at sea until I hear them again. My dad used to tell World War II stories about soldiers being so tired they fell asleep standing up, talking mid-sentence or in fox holes with bullets blazing over their heads. I never understood how that was possible until I started this job. I rest here sitting on a box until I catch myself nodding off, fingers tucked into the pockets of my hooded sweatshirt seeking warmth from the cool night air. When I start to shiver, I decide it is time to head back to my room.

As I'm putting away some letters, I hear a knock on my door. I open it to a frazzled Vanessa. I glimpse the fragility in her eyes, see the frayed edges of her being as she stands speechless in the doorway. She plops down on the sarong covered vinyl chair and comes undone. "What's up with the chief engineer?" she asks.

"I was wondering how rough he'd be on you," I say as I bite my lip.

She shifts her body in the chair, getting comfortable. "The first engineer picks me up at the airport and says I should talk with Scruggs right away. So I knock on Scruggs' door and stand there, you know, waiting for him to look up from his desk. And finally, he does. He looks up, looks right at me and says, 'Oh, for a minute I thought the new QMED was here.'"

"What?" I'm surprised and shocked that Scruggs would be so mean.

"There's more. Then I say, 'Vanessa Cantol here, sir. The new QMED.' I don't give him the satisfaction of reacting to his rudeness, and he says, 'Boy, did you jump outta the frying pan onto this ship. You'll never make it. What's a pretty lady like you doing in an engine room instead of in the galley? What makes you think you can do this?'"

Vanessa stands up, paces to the door then thumps back onto the chair.

"I told him what ships I'd been on, engines I'd taken apart and put back together. Stuff like that. And he says, 'You better always be on time and be prepared to run because you're going to be our number one gopher. And I better not hear about you sleeping with any of the engineers.'"

"'No way,' I tell him, but I'm annoyed. It's okay. I'm going to let the captain know how I was welcomed, just for the record. Know what I'm saying?" She glances at her watch. "Gotta get down there."

There has long been a semi-friendly rivalry between the mates and engineers, the jokes about people who work in the engine room. Snipes. Bilge rats. But historically, the rivalry was not friendly. It got started because ships used to be strictly sailing ships. Engineers didn't exist. But when mechanical things were put on board, a whole new breed of sailor was born: the engineer. Rumor has it that they can be a hard-headed lot.

As I get ready for bed, I think about Vanessa. Scruggs may be hard on her, but she's fighter. She'll get through it.

Talking with Vanessa is like looking in a mirror. Maybe I should have been an engineer. Here I am, bull-headed, proving to the world that I can do whatever I set out to do and along comes Vanessa, busting her buns to keep up with the big valves and the big boys. Now we are here together on an oil tanker. Two determined, out-of-money women working in a man's world.

My numb hands wake me up in the wee hours of the morning. I soak them in warm water to make the numbness go away, but now I'm awake, thinking about the past and present things like what Stanley said about climbing down the rope ladder to the launch here in Long Beach. I worry about how I am going to be able to get off this ship and into town for a night out.

When it comes time for me to go ashore the next day, the cargo has been unloaded and it's almost fifty feet from the deck down to the water. Instead of hanging vertically, the rope ladder conforms to the ship's hull and slants inward near the end making the descent even more frightening. I'm feeling a little scared about catching the launch. I'm wondering if my hands will be strong enough to hang on to the ladder.

I keep repeating in my mind what Stanley told me at breakfast. "When you're on the last rung of the rope ladder and the guy below on the launch yells, 'Now,' it's important to let go because in a split second the launch will go down and not be there to meet your foot."

"Use your legs, Jeanne. Your hands are just the guides," Stanley says when it's my turn to go down the ladder.

I hold tight and start my descent. I don't want to look down.

"That away kiddo. That's it. Use them legs," Stanley yells, like I'm a kid on a soccer team.

I am doing this. There are no problems. One foot down a rung, then second foot down. Move your hands down. Over and over I continue this pattern. The guys' voices encourage me and I repeat in my head, *Don't look down. Steady, one step at a time.*

Before I know it the guy below on the launch yells, "You're at the end. Grab my hand." Our fingers lock. I jump onto the slippery deck railing. I do it. No problem.

It's nice to be back on land, but I begin to wonder whether I am a natural born sailor. Walking to the marina, I realize that it feels weird to walk on a surface that isn't swaying back and forth. I've never once felt dizzy on the ship, even in the big swells, but I get so dizzy walking on the sidewalk that I have to stop and sit down.

In my mind I reaffirm the fact that it's great to be on land again. Sometimes when you're in the middle of the ocean with nothing around but water and an empty, flat horizon, it can get monotonous, like the feeling you had as an elementary school student in June. It's sunny and warm outside and you feel like you've already learned everything you could possibly learn for that year, yet summer vacation seems like it will never begin. You have to be there, but your mind wants something else.

The first stop on my shore leave is a coffee house by the dock. I walk through the doors, order a mocha and listen to the milk steaming machine hiss. A solo saxophonist plays a jazz tune in the background. A dog outside the door waits impatiently for its owner. The mocha glides down my throat. God it's good to be on land.

I spend the afternoon as an ordinary land woman. I shop. I try on clothes, buy a pair of jeans and a T-shirt, sample hand lotion. At the two nicest hotels I ask if the masseuse can fit me in for a massage. Neither one can.

I try to call my daughters, then Paul and Elizabeth, but when no one is home, I call my answering machine and listen to my messages. The voices of loved ones are captured on tape. I dial home again to hear their voices one more time.

I walk around until I hear a blues band playing at a sidewalk restaurant. At the bar I sway to the music, eat artichoke dip on crusty French bread and study the faces of passersby. An unexpected moment of joy hits me in the fancy ladies room when I look at all the toilet stalls and gloat over the fact that I don't have to clean so much as one of them. Not one in that gleaming dozen. I can't help but chuckle.

Before I catch the launch back to the ship, I dial my friend Elizabeth one last time. This time she answers. "There you are," she says like she always does when she hears my voice on the phone.

"I'm in Long Beach and only have ten minutes. I just want to hear your voice before I get back on the ship."

"Are you okay?" she asks.

"I'm fine."

"Is there anything we can do for you?"

"Yeah. This," I say, my voice breaking.

Now she's crying.

"They're getting on the launch now. Got to go."

"We love you."

"I love you too."

The ride back to the ship is filled with the silence of a crew returning to duty, while I carry Elizabeth and Paul's proclamation of love in my head and heart. And yet, other more difficult memories crowd in. Going ashore is bittersweet. It's a few hours of land's fleeting delights wedged between a week of the sea's eternal ones. In the darkness ahead, the silhouette of the O.S. Illinois comes into view. I can faintly make out the rope ladder and ABs walking on deck.

I climb the rope ladder with no problems and head straight to my room where I'm overcome by the memories I came out here to resolve. The dark memories sometimes overwhelm the warm, loving ones. I take out a piece of stationery and write my father a letter, another one I'll never mail.

Dear Dad,

Over the past years I've written you several letters that I haven't mailed. Here's one more. Did you get the birthday cards and Father's Day cards I sent? I never heard back.

I don't know how to say good-bye when we've never really said hello. I don't know you. Not really. And you sure as hell don't know me. What would you like to know about me? How I read every night and think about how much I love my daughters? That my favorite thing to eat in the whole world is dark chocolate? I'd like to know about the favorite tree you climbed when you were a boy and what you saw when you got to the top.

A Native American friend taught me how to send messages to you telepathically. I've been sending you those for a long time now, and I know you've gotten them. Some communications are more reliable than the mail. I've sent you love and compassion. I've tried to send understanding but couldn't because that one's not complete for me. Your life had to be pretty messed up. I just wish I knew why.

What does it feel like to lie on a bed, knowing that you're dying? What do you think about? I wish you could tell me why you did those things so I could understand.

Jeanne

Long after I fall asleep but a few hours before I begin my day, we disembark from Long Beach.

Chapter Eight

Stacking Hay

While I mop the mess halls and clean the early rooms this morning, I think about the sights and sounds of land and sea. Several guys who've been shipping for years never go ashore; they seem to prefer the routine coziness and motion of the ship. Every evening before dinner, Chuck walks into the crew mess and eats two ice cream bars. Robby always eats his soup in a paper cup so as not to dirty too many dishes. Pete has a sweet roll every morning for breakfast. The captain sneaks late night vanilla ice cream with chocolate syrup. I too have begun to develop reassuring routines, yet still, I miss, the mountains, trees, grass.

We leave Long Beach without a new dishwasher. Rich doesn't understand the why of it any more than I do.

He's called the union hall from every port, made the situation clear. Meanwhile, he continues to carry buckets full of scalding water from the pasta machine to the third sink. I continue to lift the dishes out with tongs.

We do, however, have our moments of hope. Chief Engineer Scruggs parades into the galley followed by the young third engineer. Scruggs boasts how this young man can fix anything, assures us we'll be up and running in no time. Between meals, the soft-spoken engineer works on the dishwasher, parts spread out over the galley deck, never once smiling, ever. From time to time Rich and I glance at him for a sign of his progress. We're answered with negative shakes of his head and sighs. Finally, the third engineer pronounces it hopeless.

So begins a succession of engineers who enter the galley on a mission to restore life to the dishwasher. They spend two days. They all fail. Then Scruggs steps up.

It's hard to describe how I feel today, our third day of this endeavor now, with Scruggs flat on the galley deck at my feet, cussing. My guess is we both feel strangely humbled. Scruggs takes only one day to pronounce it hopeless. He promises a new machine on our next trip to Long Beach. That's two weeks out.

I'm not there when the extraction operation takes place in the middle of the night.

I come in the next morning to find a gaping hole where the dishwasher used to be. "Scruggs and his boys yanked it," Rich says, sipping his tea. "Now, keep in mind that these guys are responsible for everything with a moving part on this tub. Generators, plumbing, water purification. They're the ones who keep this ship afloat. Uh hunh."

"Is that supposed to make me feel better?" I ask. "Because if it is, it's not working."

"Yeah, well. Let's hope they're better in the engine room then they are in the galley."

In Long Beach, we gained Vanessa, my new friend, a new third engineer and third mate, but we lost Steve, the cute bosun, Pete Third Mate Stanton and Chuck. That's the one constant of ship life: transience.

I walk into Pete's room, empty now. No picture of his fiancee on the desk, no clothes draped over the big chair. He's removed the spread and sheets from his bed, clumped them in a pile next to a twenty dollar bill. Apparently it's customary for the officers to leave tips, about a dollar for each day I clean their room.

He's also left a note. "Jeanne. I'm out of here today. Thanks for keeping my room up so nicely. Hang in there. Pete." I rub my hand over the piece of paper and place it safely in my back pocket.

I walk down to C Deck past the new third engineer's room. His door is open. He's in there unpacking. He looks like a towering fir tree, but strikes me as a gentle giant kind of guy. Early forties, big shock of golden brown hair, olive skin. He's unpacking poetry books and turns when he hears me in the passageway.

"Morning, I'm Kyle."

"Hi. Jeanne."

"Uh, don't worry too much about my room. It's pretty much always cluttered."

"Okay. I'll just hit the big, empty spots."

I glance at a guitar case, a large CD player, a shoe box filled with CDs, another box of paperback novels, two duffel bags and clothes scattered everywhere.

"Do you like music?" he asks.

"Love it."

"Have you heard this one?" He hands me the CD. It's *The Buena Vista Social Club.* "My sister gave it to me. You gotta hear it." He hands me the CD.

"You sure?" I ask him.

"Of course."

"Well, only if I can loan you one of mine."

Suddenly it hits me. I'm chatting with an officer… in his room. Time to leave.

"Gotta get busy," I say.

"Bye, Jeanne."

I run down to the galley and begin setting up for lunch in the officers' mess when Kyle comes in to eat early, because he works the noon to four P.M. watch. He's even cuter than I remember. In addition to that unusual combination of golden hair with dark brown eyes, he sports a dimple on either side of his mouth when he smiles. Mostly though, Kyle's appeal comes from an intangible quality of integrity that hovers around his six foot four inch frame. He's fascinated that I left my college teaching position to do this but says I chose the right department. Most of the guys on ships are cool about women working in the galley.

He shakes his head as he continues. "The union's created a situation where the food is standard, routine fare and when there's all guys on a ship, things gravitate to bare necessities. So when a woman shows up, the food gets a lot better. Besides, having a woman in the galley makes the place feel warmer, more like home," he says.

"But what about the deck or engine department? How are women accepted there?" I ask, filling the salt shakers.

First Mate Smiley walks in looking as if he smells a skunk and I cut our conversation short.

I'm doing dishes when some of the guys in the chow line start philosophizing about the appropriateness of women in the engine room. Vanessa's presence here has definitely sparked a controversy.

"I like to think I'm not sexist, but the truth is, women in the engine room are a problem. Too much physical strength required," QMED Brad says.

"That's why more women are mates than engineers. They don't have to use their muscles so much," a mate says.

"Yeah, those big valves and hand-holds weigh as much as an average woman. They're hard to open," another shipmate responds.

"A woman down there just creates problems. Especially when she can't do her job," Brad says.

"But what if she's strong and holds her own, you know, does the job without a guy's help?" I ask from the sink. It gets quiet really fast.

"Even if she could do the job, she'd still create a problem because guys get distracted, pay more attention to her than to what they're doing. Then someone gets hurt," Brad says.

"As if that's her responsibility," I mutter.

"Some guys are on for four months at a time, and they're all put together the same way," Brad shoots back.

I take a deep breath and let it out. "So basically, you think women shouldn't be in the engine room because of male testosterone levels? That women should be denied jobs for which they are properly trained and perfectly capable of performing, because some guy can't keep his eyes where they belong."

Now it's beyond quiet. I think no one's going to touch that one.

"You've got a point there. A good point." It's Kyle, back in the chow line for thirds. His second and third helpings endear him immediately to Rich, and when he slips his tray through the pass-through and thanks us for a great meal, Rich glows bright red.

Sugar walks up. He eats everything but the wallpaper and smells like dirty underwear. He plunks down his tray full of dirty dishes in the pass-through window. As I reach out to grab it, he retracts it. A cat and mouse deal. Only I don't play. I'm too damned tired and my hands hurt too much for this kind of game. I turn my back on the pass-through window and ignore Sugar. After a minute, he walks away and I'm able to retrieve his tray.

"That's the best thing you could have done. Start playing those boys' games and you'll never be done playing. Un hunh," Rich says.

"Jeanne," Vanessa whispers from the chow line. "Come into the crew mess for a second."

Close to tears, Vanessa sits by herself at the end of a long table. "Another scumbag QMED, that what's-his-name, Brad, started giving me crap down in the engine room this morning. I mean, I'm busting my ass opening this valve and that valve and he starts talking shit about me in front of all the guys. So I say, 'Look. I'm doing this job just like everybody else. If you don't like it, take it up with the captain. Otherwise, keep your big fat trap shut.' Jeanne, I'm telling you. That's the second guy to piss me off. What a shipload."

"Sounds like you handled it well."

"Yeah," she says, "I did, didn't I." She hugs me around the neck. "I'm so glad you're with me. Thanks for letting me vent."

"No problem. I'm always here for you," I say. Dishes clink in the pass-through. "I gotta get back in there and help Rich. Let's talk tonight at 7:30 before your watch," I tell her. She nods and I run back into the galley.

"Everything okay?" Rich asks. "That Vanessa sure doesn't eat much."

"It's okay. She's taking a beating from the guys in the engine room. No surprise," I explain.

Scruggs comes down late for lunch while Rich is in the middle of telling me a funny story about a cat who didn't know it was a cat.

Scruggs cuts in, "I got a dog for my wife... thought it was a pretty good trade."

He waits for laughter, but when we don't laugh, he storms off into the officers' mess.

"That's Scruggs. Blows hot and cold. He's stressed lately," Rich says.

I look up. "Why?"

"Two big egos on any ship." Rich waits to see if I understand. He's cleaning the grill.

I nod.

"Scruggs is sort of second in command, you know?" he says.

"A friendly rivalry between mates and engineers," I say.

"But not so friendly between Scruggs and Figarino. Scruggs and his boys keep the ship running, all systems go. Long, hard hours in a noisy, dirty engine room while the captain and his boys hang out up on the bridge. With a view."

"Maybelline," an old Chuck Berry song, is blasting away on the galley radio. It's one of Rich's favorites.

"But that's only part of it. Biggest thorn in Scruggs' side is money. He and his boys all just had pay cuts, but the captain's salary went up. Way up."

All that's left of the lunch shift is to go into the officers' mess and collect the water pitchers. Going in there usually causes a stir of some kind, but I take a deep breath and open the door.

Scruggs and the first engineer are in there talking, and it's clear by the looks on their faces that my interruption is bothersome.

"Gentlemen, I'll just get these out of your way," I say as I grab the pitchers.

"You forgot to latch open the door, Jeanne. That's about the dumbest thing you could do." Scruggs looks pleased with himself.

"How would you latch the door in this situation?" I ask, holding two water pitchers in each hand.

"I'd walk in, latch the door open, then grab the pitchers." He tilts backward, arms hinged on the chair back.

I want to kick the chair out from under him. I want to cry and throw the pitchers at his head. Instead, I set the four pitchers down on the table, latch open the door, grab the pitchers and walk out. I deliberately leave the door open. To hell with the air conditioning. To hell with giving them privacy.

When I get back to the galley with the pitchers, Rich takes one look at my face and says, "Don't ever take anything Scruggs says or does personally. He's just stressed."

"It doesn't give him license to be an asshole." I empty the water pitchers into the sink and throw my hands in the air as I walk out the door.

I climb the outside stairs to the small landing off B Deck, sit down on the corrugated metal and watch the rolling Pacific. For a moment, I wish that I could dive to the depths of the deep sea floor, far away from my own rifts. Would I find the escape I need in its hidden world of sands, subterranean mountains, plateaus and reefs? I could never do that though. As I begin to cry, I tell myself that I will face this. I cry like I did the summer I turned twelve and wanted to bale hay instead of cook the noon meal. I was swinging the bales up onto the flatbed just like the boys my age. Then all of a sudden, Dad tossed a bale down from the top of the stack right on top of me. It knocked me flat on my back. Sucked the breath right out of me. Then he told me to get back to the kitchen where I belonged. Who did I think I was? Girls can't stack hay.

Now my tears come from the fatigue of working twelve-hour days, seven days a week and from burning hands that feel like they belong to a raging, fire monster. My tears also come from the realization that I'm still out here trying to prove I'm not just a weak, stupid woman.

There's a knock on my door at 7:30. "It's open," I call out from the spot on my bed where I lie reading some letters.

Still spunky, Vanessa walks in, plops down on the chair covered in my floral throw. "Ya know. I got one kid in college and another with a new baby, but no husband. I'm supporting all of us. Do these guys think I'm out here for fun?"

"Are all ships like this?" I ask.

"No. This is my fifth ship and I've never seen this kind of attitude before," she says. "On the military ships I've been on, there's lots of women. The guys are used to us and don't give us any crap."

"Lucky us." I roll onto my side.

"This is a commercial ship with a returning crew. The guys work four months on, two months off. You and I come on as sixty-day reliefs, not part of the regular crew, and women to boot. We're stirring up the soup." She looks at her watch.

"Gotta get down there. Come on. I'll give you a tour."

We ride the elevator down four or five stories into the belly of the ship. The door opens and we are in the engine room. It's enormous and looks like a setting out of a sci-fi movie: *Vanessa and Jeanne on Planet Valve.*

"Okay, let's pretend we're following the typical day of a QMED, or, for our purposes, a new QMED named Vanessa," she says.

"When I first come down here, the QMED who's been on watch before me gives me the lowdown on what's been happening. If everything's normal, I do my visual round where I check to make sure that everything's still running smoothly. When I'm not making rounds in the pit of the engine room, I'm at the switch board watching gauges, which also show the condition of everything in the engine room."

We walk around and check things out. She takes me over to have a look at the gauges.

"The QMED takes readings on things like the boiler temperature, the feed pump, the evaporator. Keeps an eye on the cooling system, which is salt water going in and out," Vanessa explains to me.

The vastness and complexity of the engine room amaze me.

"The blue oil purifier, this bulbous round hulk, purifies the oil in the engine room then circulates it back into the system. It gets rid of any excess debris that might come in contact with the oil that's actually going through the machinery."

"Kind of like a filter?" I ask.

"Kind of. I haven't loaded and unloaded cargo on this ship yet. Cargo for us is oil. But when I do, I'll have to start up all the cargo pumps, open up a lot of steam valves and bleed the excess water out of the system. Steam coming through the lines is what activates the cargo pump."

For a moment, Vanessa stops talking and we hear only the machines. Vanessa's profile reminds me of Artemis, goddess of the hunt. Though sometimes her emotions take over, now she seems to exude confidence. She looks strong, savvy, efficient.

"Vanessa, I know you're used to diesel engines, but you're clearly in your element here," I reassure her. "You've shown the guys you can do the work. Most of them accept you. Don't worry about the ones who don't."

Open and vulnerable, she faces me. "Jeanne, you're getting me through this. I swear to God, if it weren't for you, I don't know how I'd make it to the first port."

She continues to show me around the engine room. Speechless, I stare in awe at all the gadgets, gears and machines. After we complete the tour I am even more impressed with the job Vanessa does.

As I take my leave, Kyle, who has just finished his

overtime hours, rides up in the elevator with me. We stop at B Deck and he lingers a bit longer than I expect him to, regaling me with stories from the trenches.

"You come out of the hole wiped out. Twelve hours of that heat takes a toll on you," he says.

I watch him speak but don't hear what he says, because I'm thinking, *That's it. That's who he looks like. Brad Pitt.*

We stand there all awkward-like until I say the next thing that pops into my head. "I noticed you read poetry."

"Especially Neruda, but I forgot my copy," he says.

"I have a copy in my room. Spanish on one side, English on the other."

"I speak Spanish. My mother is Mexican." He grins.

"Well then, I'll leave my copy in your room. Have a good night," I say. When I turn away, my hand accidentally brushes his.

He steps off the elevator. "Thanks so much and good night to you too," he says, still smiling as the door closes between us.

I remind myself that I didn't come out here to meet a man. I'm here to begin a new adventurous career, gain financial independence and have time to create. Besides, I probably wouldn't have much in common with an engineer anyway. I hear Fred York's advice from the union hall about ships and sexual relationships. Right now, I wish I hadn't listened.

After finding my copy of Neruda and leaving it in Kyle's room, I decide to go for my afternoon walk out on the deck. Once again, there are some porpoises riding the waves. I love to watch them swim around. It seems like they have so much fun. Robby is also on deck and joins me in observing the delightful creatures. We stand on the bow and watch as they catch a wave. Their faces look as though they're smiling up at us. Robby says they're just playing, but to me, it looks like they're racing the ship to see who's faster. It's a close race, but those porpoises always come out ahead.

We arrive in Valdez during a late evening shower. Even in rain, it's beautiful. The majestic mountains, the lush green moss met by rock and snow. A powerful peace descends as I take it all in.

We'll leave after lunch tomorrow with barely enough time to get our mail and make phone calls home. No time to go ashore. No time, either, for the new mate who showed up with a bottle of wine in his backpack to join the ship in Valdez. He was fired on the spot. One thing they don't kid about or take lightly is mixing alcohol with oil tankers in Valdez.

As I'm heading into the house to find my phone card, Robby walks toward me carrying one letter and a package. "For you," he says.

I rush back to my room where I can savor my mail in private. I can tell from the handwriting that it is from Lisa, my younger daughter.

Hi Mom,

All my friends want to meet you. They can't believe that you quit teaching to work on a ship. They say their parents would never do anything so wild. My friend Carey said her mom's big adventure is to plan for a two week vacation once a year, so if I haven't ever said so straight out, I want to say it now—thanks for giving me the courage to follow my dreams.

Hanging out at the Union Hall waiting for a job sounds trippy. What a great time to catch up on sketching and writing little observations. Knowing you, you've also paid all your bills and organized your paper work for the next ten years. Life at sea must be totally different from the life of academia that you're used to, but I am sure you are doing great.

Mom, I love you and miss you more than I thought possible. I cannot wait to see you.

Love,

Lisa

I am so lucky to have such loving daughters, I think to myself as I gently fold the letter back into the envelope and place it in my desk drawer. I wonder what is going on with Emily until I see that the return address for the package is from my older daughter. I cannot wait to see what is inside. I rip the tape off the top of the box to find an envelope. Inside is a card with a tuxedo black and white kitty on the front. On the cat's white chest Emily has written the name of her cat: Boris. The cover reads, "I spend a lot of time thinking about you," while on the inside it says, "It helps me kill time in between meals." I laugh. Getting mail from both of my daughters on the same day is a Godsend. Life can't get any better.

I rummage through the white Styrofoam peanuts in the package. Next thing I know I am pulling out peppermint foot treatment, high intensity hand treatment, body lotion, peppermint body wash and an assortment of chocolates. There are milk chocolate hazelnut truffles, dark chocolate candy bars, milk chocolate with peanut butter and chocolate covered praline almonds. This is heaven! I sniff each of the lotions and then start to try some of them out. I debate whether or not to try the foot and hand treatments right away, but decide to hold off until later. The chocolates seem to be calling my name so I eat two glorious pieces, one of the chocolate with peanut butter and the other a piece of dark chocolate.

I lay down on my bed feeling like I am a child that just finished opening the gifts Santa has brought on Christmas. I am filled with happiness as I gaze at the photos of my daughters I brought in my luggage. I vividly remember when the doctor first handed them to me. Pure joy. Remembering the days of their births, looking over the messages they sent, savoring the taste of the chocolate in my mouth and smelling the lotions I put on my hands, brings me to a wonderful place.

Our first day out of Valdez we have our weekly fire and boat
drills. Stanley and two other ABs lead team two, but Stanley
starts to shake so badly that he can't put the big plastic fire
hat on his head. I'm not sure why he's shaking. Perhaps it is
pressure of performing in front of his peers or maybe the
power of alienation is taking its toll. I'm relieved when one
of the ABs offers him a hand.

I pay close attention while I help Rich and Al put out
a pretend fire on the bridge. Figarino and the second mate
supervise while the three of us stand on the same side of the
heavy hose and aim it into the sea. After the drill, Rich holds
up the middle so that the water drains out both ends.

Next is the boat drill, the practice for abandoning
ship in the two life boats. My boat is port side with the new
bosun and the new third mate, Donny. Rich calls him Dandy
Donny. Apparently they've sailed together before.

At the conclusion of these drills one person must
don the hooded, footed dry suit we stow in our rooms in a
stuff sack. Its purpose is to keep us dry and warm in case we
end up in the water. Today the new bosun points to Rich.

"No way, man. I wore that thing the last drill," he says.

When Rich wore it last week, Robby had to help
him into it. Robby's the only one I've seen so far who can put
on the dry suit by himself. And so, today, I get the honors.

Robby helps me carry it down from my room. "Too
heavy for your sore hands," he says, laying the dry suit down
on the deck.

"Now sit down and push your boots into it. Boots keep you warm." He helps me stand and squeeze into the hood, which pulls at my hair. It's claustrophobic and the range of motion is limited, but I've passed the test. I'm successfully in the dry suit.

At the end of the drill with my hands closed inside rubber mitts, I find it impossible to get out of the suit alone. Robby helps. He hesitates to unzip me down the front, but finally reaches for the long black pull tab, yanks it down and, a bit flustered, he walks away. Not an officer, but certainly a gentleman.

Chapter Nine

Tattoo

This afternoon, on our first day out of Valdez, I notice two tiny brown shore birds blown out to sea by the wind. They look like sparrows, only longer and thinner. One lies dead on the deck. I gently pick it up by its belly and bury it at sea. The other one struggles to escape the ship's domain. Her wings flap fast as blinks: glide, flutter, flap. But no matter how she tries, she can't fly away.

"I feel sorry for the birds who get confused and end up on this ship so far away from home," I say to Rich later while we stand at the sinks.

"Shore birds are like you, Jeanne." His face looks serious.

"Well, I'm tougher than I look."

"Gotta hand it to ya. Didn't want to say anything till now. But when you first got on, the crew was making bets as to how long you'd last."

"Is that a fact?"

"Oh, that's a fact."

I'm on the stern after dinner watching the scene behind the ship when it hits me again. We're 600 miles from the coast, in the middle of nothing but water. Out here, there's only the sea, the ship and the crew. My spirit seeks its compass as we move on. Two white-gray birds rise into sight and follow close behind this solitary ship. Albatross. Bodies noticeably fuller, more substantial than seagulls, albatross glide side-to-side, never flapping, just coasting. I wonder, this far out to sea, where they sleep.

Tonight the sea looks calm, sleepy, thick like a warm blanket. There are no waves as we sail toward Port Angeles, where we'll pick up the pilot who will take us north through Rosario Strait past the San Juan Islands to Anacortes, then on to Bellingham. Rich is all fired up because his wife will join the ship in Bellingham; I'm all fired up, because Al will be getting off there. The sunset is cream white against dark, purple-gray puff clouds and a patch of blue sky behind flatter, softer gray clouds.

Back in my room, I dive into my pajamas and peer out my porthole. A huge silvery moon rises over the watery horizon. A swollen full moon that gives me pause. I want to go outside, take a picture, but that would mean getting dressed again. The fatigue of the day has hit me hard. I close the curtain, lie down and try to sleep. But it's no use; even behind my closed eyelids I still see that incredible corpulent moon.

Before I know it, my alarm clock sounds and another day begins. An hour later I've mopped the mess halls, done a load of wash and cleaned three showers before I walk into my room to put away my clean clothes. I open the curtain to a peachy-orange sun rising over the churning water. I walk out the steel door and snap a picture of the scene. Maybe I'll catch sight of that wondrous moon tonight. But right now, I'm content to have this ten-minute morning break. I haven't done it before, but for a moment, I sit and do nothing.

Later in the morning we're in really rough seas: twenty-five-foot swells. On this 800-foot long tanker it feels like being in an amusement park fun house where the floors slant and you lose your balance. I'm not sick, just constantly hungry; if I have food in my stomach, I feel fine.

Rich laughs at how much I eat for breakfast in these swells: a three-egg Denver omelet, a short stack, cantaloupe, juice and two cinnamon rolls slathered with melted butter. They've done studies about the caloric intake of sailors and found that during rough seas like this, with all the energy it takes to stay upright while the deck heaves to and fro, we need four thousand calories a day. I'm in the zone.

In these swells the ship is taking extra knocks that precipitate machinery problems everywhere. The engineers are working overtime on top of their overtime.

With working eleven, sometimes twelve to thirteen hour days, all inside the ship, mostly without portholes, whenever I have a moment, I go outside and gaze at the sea. Now that the decks are closed from the rough weather, I can't go outside at all. All of the outdoors I can see is from the portholes, and because we're rolling side-to-side, the color of the water mixes with the sky. People who haven't spent a lot of time at sea think it's like being at the beach, watching the ocean from land, but it isn't like that at all. When you are on a ship for so long it feels like you are one with the ocean. Every wave, every movement is felt in every corner of the ship. It is inescapable. Day and night, night and day, you feel the ocean like your own heart beating. Sometimes it's pretty, calming, soothing, other times its violent and churning. One thing it certainly isn't, is a day at the beach.

I'm cleaning rooms, and I fly past Scruggs' normally closed door. He stands at his desk, back turned toward the open door, wearing nothing but his T-shirt and red plaid boxer shorts. He's reading a memo.

"Morning, Chief," I mutter as I walk past.

"There's going to be a drill," he mutters back.

Scruggs is in charge this time. It's held in the steering gear room located in the stern, three flights below the upper deck. We already had our weekly drill; this one catches everyone off guard.

I had no idea the steering gear room even existed but I find it fascinating. It's the ship's version of a doll house with its miniature helm for emergency situations when the bridge helm might be inoperable.

The crew crowds in around Scruggs, who stands beside an array of gadgets, buttons, levers and lights. It's so noisy I can't even hear my own voice when I ask Robby a question. He can't hear me either and pantomimes a hilarious response.

Scruggs has to shout. "If you're the guy down here when the phone rings and it's the bridge calling down to tell you to take over the steering, this is what you do. Walk around this pole, flip this switch on the back that disengages the steering from the bridge to down here, and then steer with this little wheel. Got that?" He looks around at each crew member.

Then he asks for a volunteer to demonstrate, to make sure we've been listening. The image of his red plaid boxer shorts flashes through my mind. I avoid eye contact and hope he doesn't pick me. Scruggs reaches out and grabs the person closest to him. Rich.

Rich's face looks wagon red against his white hair, but I have faith in him. I know he can do it. I know he'll show the rest of the crew that we in the steward department have what it takes to steer a ship. Rich steps up to the controls, his eyes moving from lever to button to wheel to phone to pole. The phone rings.

It's Captain Figarino calling from the bridge. We hear his voice come over the loudspeaker, saying, "I'm disengaging the steering devise from the bridge." It sounds like Mickey Mouse talking into a tin can, only tinier. I have visions of him standing behind a curtain to our right, talking into a mouse megaphone.

Rich goes into action. He walks around the pole and flips the switch to steering gear control. He pushes the button, pulls the lever and proceeds to adjust the mini-wheel. When he over-steers, I start to get nervous and imagine we're no longer cutting into the waves properly, and we're broadsided by a big one. Scruggs looks nervous too, looks like he's not breathing. About then our most experienced AB steps up to help. Stanley's eyes hold the pain and longing of the world as he grips the mini-helm, checks all the gauges and makes the proper adjustments. In less than a minute, we're under control, back on course. A shadow of a grin curls on the corners of Stanley's mouth, like the Mona Lisa.

The phone rings. It's the captain. "Good job. Get back to work."

Back in the galley, Rich is stirring lemon cake batter when I applaud him for a job well done. "You represented the steward department with style and class," I say.

"Well, I was sweating like a stuck pig, 'cause I didn't hear one word the chief said down there in that disco. I only saw the knobs he pushed. But I remembered them all and pushed the same ones."

Meanwhile, Al, his plumber butt in full view, stands in his dirty khakis at the sink during lunch prep and piles up six or seven inches of potato peels, celery ends and onion skins, then runs the disposal. When his mess backs up, he smiles a wicked one like I've never seen him smile. He's delighted. In a moment of pure joy, he blames the mayhem on me.

"Jeanne, I keep telling you to run the disposal more often."

"Yeah, well I guess you better start telling yourself," I say.

All three sinks spring leaks. Putrid gray water travels down under the salad bar, pools in the corner next to the refrigerators and trays. There is so much water on the galley deck that Rich mops all through lunch to prevent us from slipping and falling.

The engineers go crazy. They're the ones who have to clean the wretched, stinking drains. The galley smells like a chemistry experiment gone bad.

"Has someone been sick?" Figarino asks at lunch. "It smells like vomit in the passageway."

"No sir," Al says. "Backed up sinks. We think Jeanne's glove liner went down the drain."

He looks from the captain to me to the stinking sink. Now all he lacks in order to play the perfect villain is a waxed, handlebar mustache.

"Either that or Al's ass," I grumble.

A day later we're on the hook in Port Angeles, where I first boarded the O.S. Illinois. I take the afternoon launch in search of someone who can help fix my aching hands, but it's Sunday. Doctors are scarce. The launch fellow directs me to a masseuse who works in some old-fashioned steam baths in one of the oldest buildings in town. These baths were built in the 1920s when the United States was thinking of having two national capitals: one in the east, one here in Port Angeles. The western capitol was to have all the great amenities.

A long hallway leads to individual steam rooms. Mine has the original tiled walls, steps that lead to a top tier, a long string to pull for more steam. My hostess walks in as I am surveying the room and says, "Set the timer for thirty minutes, drink lots of water and signal that you're finished by removing the big, fat terry cloth robe from the hook in the hallway."

The steam room is at least twelve by fifteen feet with seven steps up to the top tier where I lie for almost the entire thirty minutes. When I get too hot, I either plunge my feet in the bucket of cold water she's filled for me, or walk down the seven steps and take a cold shower. It's the best steam of my life. I lie there naked on my back, my stomach flat. After weeks on the ship it's concave again like when I was younger and thinner. It feels good to experience that sensation again. I lie there and breathe deep breaths. I inhale slowly and exhale out the same way. When a thought enters my mind, whether good or bad, I visualize it floating up and away on a cloud of steam. I stay with my breath, stay with being in my body. So far, the easiest ways for me to accomplish this feat have been dancing, meditation and yoga.

The ritual of private steam, pulling the string for more steam, lying down to sweat, sitting up and plunging my feet into cold water, lying down to sweat again, walking down the steps and taking a cold shower, is one of the most pleasurable experiences I've had in a month. These actions remind me to treasure this wonderful body I have been given, to treat it tenderly, to honor it as the house of my spirit. When the thirty minute timer rings, I shower and drink another cup of water before I lift the robe from the hallway, snuggle into its warmth and wait for my turn. I cannot believe how good I feel right now. I am totally relaxed, invigorated and almost pain-free, and I haven't even been massaged yet. I snuggle into the robe, ready for part two.

My hostess, Tami, gives me a magnificent massage. We talk for a while, in which time she asks me what I do on the tanker. I give her the headlines about the broken dishwasher, about the numbness, swelling and pain in my hands.

"All men on the ship?" she asks. "No female energy," she continues, not waiting for an answer.

"I really miss having women to talk with," I confess.

When Tami moves from my back to rub my feet and ankles, I immediately begin to cry. I cry through the rest of the massage. She is kind enough to call around town and find a chiropractor who will see me later this evening. She sets the appointment for 6:30, right after I finish my evening duties. Actually it is perfect timing, because I forgot that the captain, bless his heart, had arranged for a special transport for the steward staff this evening just after six o'clock.

On my way back to the ship I call my daughters and friends, but no one's home. I listen to their messages, and although it makes me happy to hear their voices from miles and miles away, they are the same messages I've heard over and over. I'm inside the phone booth thinking about how some people do this work all their lives. Home two months, at sea for four, and so on. Lonesome. For born sailors, their ship is their home. I don't feel like that, and yet tonight, for this one particularly homesick evening, the O.S. Illinois is my home. I board the launch disheartened but refreshed for my evening duties. They actually pass very quickly, a testament to the steam ritual and the massage.

I catch the steward launch shortly after dinner, hail a cab and make it to the chiropractor's office five minutes late. The doctor greets me wearing a white coat over blue jeans

and a sweater. He is of medium build with graying hair and
has a pleasant smile. Mostly though, he is gentle. He's not
pushy and helps me tremendously, not only with the adjustments, but also with stretches to do on my own. He even
gives me a new sleeping position that should help relieve
some tension in my muscles. After the session, he calls a cab
for me, but when they say it will be about twenty to thirty
minutes, he offers me a ride to my destination. I ask to be
dropped off at a restaurant I saw close to the transport. A few
people said it has good music and clams, my favorite.

The restaurant is actually a new brewery in town and
when I enter, I figure I will get served quicker sitting at the
bar. Despite what I heard, there is no live music tonight and
they're out of clams. The woman I am sitting next to mentions to me that I should try the mussels. That is exactly
what I do. In lieu of clams I order the mussels. In lieu of
music, I talk to Jenn, the woman sitting next to me.

Turns out that Jenn is the bartender's wife and one
of their beers carries the name she gave it. We talk about
everything from kids to pets, to multiple sclerosis, to auto-
immune diseases, her career in geology, my work on the ship
and her move from California to Port Angeles. We chat from
seven to nine o'clock or so. She glances at the clock over the
bar and says, "I've got to go. It's been nice talking with you."
As she heads into the kitchen, I leave the restaurant and
return to the ship for an early night.

Heading straight for my room, I debate whether it is better to go to bed early or write to my daughters and friends. Since I was unable to get in touch with them today, I decide to write to them. When I finally get to my cabin I grab my journal, rip some pages out of it and begin writing the letters. First I write my daughters:

Port Angeles
Dear Emily and Lisa,

First, thanks for the letters and package. You have no idea how much they meant to me. It is always wonderful to hear from you. I miss you both very much.

Guess what? I'm no longer the only woman on the O.S. Illinois. Before we left Long Beach, we picked up Vanessa. She's a QMED in the engine room. She's also a strong Texan who has become a great friend of mine in the short time she has been aboard. We meet up regularly during our breaks and discuss what is happening on this ship. She recently gave me a tour of the engine room. It was amazing. There were switches and levers everywhere. I don't know how anyone can remember what switch does what job and how everything works.

Well, I just wanted to drop a quick note. How's work going by the way? I want to hear all about it in your next letters. I miss you.

Love,
Mom

When I finish this letter I stare at Lisa and Emily's pictures. I miss them dearly. Then I look at the picture of Elizabeth and Paul and though I'm feeling tired, I write a letter to them as well.

Port Angeles
Dear Elizabeth and Paul,

I know you've both visited Port Angeles before, but it's worth reminding you of how beautiful the land is—the mountains, the water and the evergreen forests. I keep thinking of how spectacular it must have been before all the buildings and highways were here. It's kind of funny to be back where I started, but I didn't have time to sightsee that first night.

Last night after dinner I took the steward department launch into town in search of a massage and a good dinner. For me it was all about getting off the ship, relaxing and not eating any ship food. I feel like royalty whenever I get off the ship and walk around on land all cleaned up in street clothes instead of in my twelve-hour-a-day grubbies. Being massaged and waited on in a restaurant makes me feel positively giddy. I've been leaving really big tips lately. I went into this place that's supposed to have live music and the best clams in town, but as it turned out, the music was canceled and they were out of clams. The mussels were terrific though. You'd love 'em, Paul.

While I was there, I got to know a woman who turned out to be the bartender's wife. She actually named one of the beers

*that was served there. She saw how disappointed I was about
the music so she told me about a place called The Crossroads,
where live music is played almost every night. I plan on going
tomorrow. I wish you guys were here so we could go together.
We'd have so much fun.*

    *I think of you both all the time. Hope you're both doing well.
Love and good thoughts,*
Jeanne

As I finish signing my name, my eyelids start to close. They
have been heavy since I started writing. With no reason to
fight my weariness any longer, I quickly get under the covers
and let sleep come.

In the chow line this morning Donny, the stocky new third
mate, married with three kids, comes through with a giant
smile on his face. He has brown hair and hazel eyes, and
reminds me of a wrestler. He's got that All-American, over-
muscled athletic look that high school girls go crazy over.
Personally, it's never done a thing for me. He winks at me
coyly. I'm not in the mood for games this morning so I ignore
him.

    Later, I'm walking up the stairwell as Donny and the
second mate are walking down. "Well, what are you going to

do, Donny?" the second mate asks loudly. "Write your wife and tell her you're sleeping with Jeanne?"

"Don't listen to this devil," Donny calls, cupping his hands over the second's mouth.

"In your wildest dreams," I retort.

As if that's not enough, while I'm in the stock room before lunch, standing on the biggest box, moving other boxes around so I can get to the one in back with the cases of toilet paper, up strolls Dandy Donny.

He lifts weights. His legs are so beefed up he walks straddle-legged. He eats mostly protein, stuff like cans of tuna and egg whites, which give him that constipated look. Rich says one time Donny ate twenty-three tacos.

"Would you like to meet in town for drinks after dinner?" he asks.

I do a double-take. "What?"

"I'm having dinner with Scruggs and the port captain, but you and I could meet some place later."

"No thanks," I say to him. "I've got plans."

As if he hasn't heard me, he winks like we have a date and walks out of the stock room.

"You've got problems," I mutter, shaking my head.

I haven't told Robby about Donny's weirdness, but it's as though he knows. At lunch while I'm bent over the deep middle sink, I look over my left shoulder toward the chow line and there stands Robby, his dark brown eyes full of compassion. This time rather than cleaning supplies or medicine, he gives me the invisible gift of encouragement. As always, when I see him, I feel as if I'm in the presence of a holy man. Just knowing he's on the ship makes me feel like everything will be fine.

It's our last night in Port Angeles—I'm going out to The Crossroads. I strike a deal with a cab driver. He is going to take me out there, pick me up at 11:00 P.M. and drive me back to catch the launch for a nice tip. If I miss the launch, the next one's at 4:00 A.M. I will never survive tomorrow if that happens. The cab driver takes me twelve miles out of town to what he and Jenn, the bartender's wife I met yesterday, call the best place for live music around. He pulls up in front of a dilapidated, rough-hewn structure teetering on the edge of a cliff overlooking Puget Sound. Several Harleys are wedged between raised-bed pickups with jumbo tires.

"Don't worry," the driver says when he sees the look on my face in his rearview mirror. "They're a nice bunch of people. The guy who owns the place is an expert in martial arts. Never lets it get rough. Everybody knows it. One time he says to me, 'Bob. Try to hit me. Go ahead. Give it all you've got.' Next thing I know my hands are up over my head and he's standing there smiling at me."

Old bikers, cowboys, hippies and sailors fill the smoky tavern. I sit near the stage and let the music take me where it will.

A short while later in the dark, smoke-filled room, I see the dim figure of a guy with a long, dark ponytail walk in and head for the pool tables in the back. Once or twice I feel his eyes on me. I remember the crush of the huge, rolling wave that knocked me to the deck as I walked the windward side, remember the concerned look on the bosun's face as I made my way back to the house and it hits me. The pony-tailed guy making his way across the room to where I'm sitting is Steve, our first bosun.

"Hey. How ya doing?" Steve says and sits down.

"Steve, what are you doing here?"

"New ship's dock side, ironing out mechanical problems. You guys are out on the hook. Saw you come in."

We catch up on news, shoot pool. Being with Steve feels like being out with a kid brother. Safe. Comfortable. He plans on closing the place down, because he doesn't have a launch to catch, but my carriage turns into a pumpkin at eleven when the cabby finds me in the crowded room.

"Here ya go," Steve says to the driver and hands him a twenty.

"No way. I've got it," I say.

"Relax," Steve says. "Keep it. You work hard for your money."

"Thanks."

"Sweet dreams."

Sweet dreams. In the back of the cab a dream I had before I shipped out pops into my mind. *I see a rose and the merchant marine logo tattooed on my hands before I realize the marks will be on my skin forever.*

Chapter Ten

Unchain My Heart

We leave Port Angeles and head for Anacortes. We sail through Rosario Straits while the amber sun sets behind islands covered with firs, spruce and hemlock. Boulders grace the water's edge and cormorants swoop down over the bow.

It's late when Al, Rich and a salty old QMED hold court outside my room. They've been having happy hour. Al's getting off the ship in Bellingham and wants to store some of his gear in the linen closet which adjoins my room. Rich is along for the ride. The tag-along QMED just wants some old towels for the engine room. I'm heading toward my room just in time.

"She's got it locked," Al says to Rich. He's sweating profusely and scratching his crotch.

"Of course I've got it locked. It leads to my room," I say when I hear the commotion. The three of them practically jump out of their skins. They all have looks of guilt on their faces like they've been caught with their hands in a cookie jar.

Rich is wearing his blue coverall Arctic suit because, at the captain's request, he's doing inventory in the walk-in freezer and cooler. Apparently, he forgot to order lowfat milk for Figarino, who saves his fat intake for ice cream and chocolate.

I unlock the linen locker door, watch as Rich hands the QMED one of the big bags destined for the trash heap that I've filled with the old tattered sheets and towels. Stunned, I continue to watch as Al rifles through another, also clearly meant for the garbage dump, then holds up a natty towel, four stained sheets and ripped laundry bags all with dark orange stains.

"What's wrong with these? They're just a little rusted," Al says.

"What? Are you serious?" I ask.

"With all the guys on this ship, we can't throw things away just because they're rusted," Al goes on. I see now that he's flat-assed drunk.

"Would any of you want these on your beds?" I ask.

No one replies. I'm surprised Rich doesn't back me, until I realize he's not going to do it and look less manly to Al.

Al and Rich continue to pull stuff out of bags, throwing various items onto neat piles of sheets, towels, bedspreads and blankets that took me days to organize.

"You're gonna have to do a linen inventory," Al slurs. "We used to go five weeks without dropping off linens in port. This last time was just two weeks."

"Look Al. We can still go five weeks. We'll just have to use some of the white flat sheets usually reserved for the guys in the officers' quarters toward the end. We were doing that when I first got on."

"No way. We had enough colored sheets for the officers for five straight weeks."

"Really? Were you changing the linens?"

"Whatever. You still need to do an inventory," Al says with a sneer. Then he waves his index finger in a circle beside his ear to indicate to the others just how crazy I must be.

When the three of them get into a heated discussion about the captain, I figure it's a good time to leave. I walk the fours steps to my room, open the door and go inside, wishing I'd told them where they could put their inventory. If I went into the galley and started messing up their pots and pans, questioning why this was here and that was there, they'd have my ass in a sling.

The following day, Rich says his customary good morning while I mop and he preps for breakfast. I return the greeting, but that's all I say. Both he and Al tiptoe around me all morning while I wait for one of them to mention inventory or the linen locker or whatever. They don't say one word.

Al gets off the ship for good after lunch. I shed no tears.

In Anacortes, Dave, the tall robust new cook, comes on board. Much to my relief, he's the complete opposite of Al. Dave's a clean-shaven, big-hearted, Paul Bunyan kind of Northwest man who says what he means and means what he says. He's totally without sarcasm, cynicism and doesn't have a passive-aggressive bone in his body. His wife Marcy drove from central Washington to meet him; they're newlyweds, but nevertheless, Dave ships out tomorrow without her. Marcy is also a mariner and will board her own ship within a week. After that, they won't see each other for four months.

The three of us go out on the town. We order oyster shooters and fried clams, but Marcy isn't hungry. She looks sad as she holds Dave's hand and peers deep into his eyes. Then she tells me the story of how they met while working on a cruise ship in Hawaii.

"Your friend is here," Dave interrupts.

"Who?" I ask as I scan the crowded room.

Dave points to Kyle who is all gussied up in a black turtle neck and jeans. Kyle returns the greeting with a wave and joins us at the bar, where, after introductions and small talk, the newlyweds start kissing. Kyle and I figure that's our cue to give them privacy.

We're standing on the sidewalk talking about where we want to go next when a taxi pulls up. Robby is in the back. He's wearing a red and yellow flowered shirt, clean jeans and a yellow and green striped bandanna on his head. He's been drinking, but except for the continuous swearing, which only happens when he's under the influence, he's as sweet as ever. He's smiling like a fat Buddha.

"I brought this goddamned cab for you fucking assholes so we can go to a better place," he says. "This place sucks."

While the sun sets over Puget Sound, the cabby drives us downtown along the waterfront past antique stores and coffee shops and stops in front of a seafood restaurant where Kyle and I attempt to pay the driver. Robby won't hear of it.

"Put away your damn money." He pulls out his silver and turquoise money clip, waves a twenty dollar bill in the air. Then hands it to the cabby and tells him to take out an ample tip. Afterwards, the three of us head for the front door of the restaurant.

We're barely seated in tall, cushy bar chairs when Robby excuses himself. "Gotta go buy some presents for my daughters."

Kyle and I drink merlot. We share a platter of calamari and wonderful conversation. We talk about kids, their great energy, how they give so much more than they take, how they love unconditionally. We talk about poetry. Kyle is paraphrasing a Neruda poem about the sea when Scruggs, Smiley, Donny, and the port captain walk in.

Scruggs and Donny give us dirty looks as they're shown to a table. We have a clear view of them and can't help but notice when Scruggs glances over at us, then whispers something to Donny. Kyle turns his back to their table. I tell him the obnoxious and creepy stuff Donny said earlier about sleeping with me.

"Most of these guys have been on ships long enough to know what's true and what isn't. Guys like Robby, Rich and I know who you are," Kyle says.

What a great guy, I think to myself. He's smart, kind, well-read and cute. If I met him in other circumstances, I'd be open to the possibility of romance, but with things as they are and with Fred York's lecture burning a hole in my brain—*treat every guy the same way*—I have to close my heart.

We're laughing about Donny's ridiculous antics when Dandy Donny strolls up behind us. He scopes out Kyle like a boxer stares at his opponent across the ring. He glares at me like a jealous lover.

Donny slaps Kyle hard on the shoulder with one hand. "How ya doing, buddy," he says, while his other hand runs a finger down my back.

I jump down from my tall chair as if burned by his touch. Donny and Kyle look hard at each other, then Donny swaggers off toward the restroom.

Now the other officers at the table stare at us as if we're on stage.

"Let's get the hell out of here," Kyle says. "Karaoke time."

We're paying the calamari tab when Robby returns, fifty dollar bill in hand and the three of us exit much like The Three Musketeers. Together, and with a flourish.

"I'll send the goddamned cab driver back for you fucking guys," Robby says when we get to the karaoke place. "Some of us gotta work."

Kyle orders drinks while we leaf through the song book.

"You gotta have big balls to do Karaoke," he says. "And we've got big balls."

Kyle's double Manhattan arrives, its dark red cherry sunken down in the amber whiskey. Cigarette and Manhattan in hand, much like an old-fashioned crooner, Kyle takes the stage. He cradles the microphone and belts out "Unchain My Heart." He receives a wild round of applause.

Ten minutes later, bright yellow under the street lamps, our cab arrives. "Your friend Robby told me to come back and get you," the driver says. "Put away your money. Robby already paid."

Halfway to the ship we get hungry again and stop at a convenience store for a candy fix. We choose two yellow packs of peanut M&Ms and a box of Junior Mints and eat in the backseat of the cab all the way back to the dock where we walk under, over and through the maze of pipes, walk-ways and grates.

"It's hard to know where to walk," I say.

"That's okay. Stick with me," Kyle says, as he wraps his long arm across my shoulders, pulling me close to his side.

His touch moves me. I want to fold into him, lean against his chest.

"We better not get closer. I don't trust myself," I say, and ever so reluctantly, pull away.

"Oh, I like being close to you," he says. He looks dis-heartened.

"Kyle, you're great. It's just that a ship isn't a good place to get involved," I hear myself say. But I'm confused whether or not I really mean it.

"Yeah. Small community and all."

"Tiny," I say.

"But poetry and music. We can still talk about that."

I nod. We shake on it.

In my room I read part of "Keeping Quiet," a Neruda poem.

> let's stop for one second,
> and not move our arms so much.
> It would be an exotic moment
> without rush, without engines;
> we would all be together
> in a sudden strangeness.

It reminds me of the magic moment of relating to another person, like the one I just had. It reminds me of Kyle.

Valdez truly boasts her natural beauty this trip. She bombards you with her glory from the snow that lightly covers her mountains to the glaciers that creep down crevasses toward the deep blue sea and the reflection of the shining sun off of everything that surrounds you.

It's freezing cold when Vanessa and I call a cab from the over-sized phone booth containing three, sit-down mini booths. While we wait, Vanessa dials home to Texas, talks with one of her daughters and I gaze out at the snow, the ships docked across the bridge, the road that leads away to freedom.

Our cab finally arrives and takes us into downtown Valdez. Vanessa has less than two hours before her four o'clock watch so she asks the cabbie to return to pick her up. She wants to talk and get away from the ship for a little while, so we find a cafe where we sit on our buns and order mocha lattes and three kinds of cookies. She talks about her ex-boyfriend.

"That last time, he hit me so hard on the back of the head that I got two black eyes from it," Vanessa says.

"Please promise me you'll never speak with him again," I say.

She looks down and stares into her coffee cup. "I know, you're right."

"It's a progressive thing. If there's a next time, he'll hit you even harder and eventually, he'll kill you."

"I know. I know. I know you're right because that last time, when my head was hitting the wall, then the floor, and when he was kicking me in the stomach and back, suddenly reality set in and I thought, *He's killing me. I have to get outta here because he's killing me.*"

Vanessa's cab pulls up and she starts crying. "Don't worry, Jeanne. I'm okay," she says.

Like so many of us, Vanessa is searching for a way to value herself. It's a difficult lesson, one that takes some of us a good stretch of time to learn. I take out my notebook and write down a list of things that once helped a college student of mine who confided in me.

- Make a list of names he called you. Make another list of names your loved ones and friends call you. Compare lists. Take in the truth.
- Write two stories: one about where your life will be in five, ten and twenty years if you go back with him; one about where your life will be in five, ten and twenty years if you take a new direction.
- Write a letter addressed to your daughter as if she were the one who had experienced his violence. Tell her why you don't ever want her to talk with him again. Put the letter away for a month, take it out and change the salutation to, "Dear Vanessa."

- Write a list of all the loving things you do and say for your children and friends. Begin to do and say at least one of those each day for yourself.
- Write a poem in which you compare yourself to a star, a sunrise, a sunset, a pearl, a diamond, an amethyst, a ruby, an emerald or a sapphire.
- Write a poem in which you describe the way your face looked after he hit you the last time. Write how it felt to look like that, to feel like that.
- Write a journal entry describing your strengths, another describing his weaknesses. Write about why he needs you so much.
- Write about what you think it would be like to be with a man who was kind to you, loved you unconditionally for who you are, not because of what you can do for him.

I finish writing the note to Vanessa, then walk in the freezing afternoon rain to Mike's Palace, a seafood restaurant Rich recommended. The place is deserted this time of day, but the server says I can drink as much tea as I want until the place fills up for dinner. I savor each sip of my Earl Grey along with every minute I'm free to do nothing. When they don't have to perform hard manual labor, my hands start to feel a little better.

My server's name is Dana. A young woman in her late twenties, she is living with her sister in Alaska while she works at the restaurant for the summer. She sits down across from me in the empty restaurant and tells me how her father's death this past year has made her rethink her life. She's decided to stay the winter in Alaska, live here for four full seasons, take time to grieve her father's death and restructure her own life.

"I don't want to waste any part of my life. It's too short," she says.

I think about my father and his life ebbing. I think about my own life and where I want it to take me.

When I return to the O.S. Illinois, I find a letter from Elizabeth resting beside my door. I tear it open.

Dear Jeanne,

I woke up this morning knowing that I need to tell you the dream I had about you.

You were parked in a beat-up old car, taking a rest during a long road trip, when I came walking alongside. We both waved, and then your car started to roll backwards down a steep hill. You called out, "Help. There are no brakes."

Then I woke up.

I sense that you're giving yourself away again. Not to a relationship like you've done before, but to the work on the ship. You're still so hungry for love and acceptance that you run to catch the slightest crumb that anyone drops. Part of you still thinks that crumbs are enough. You're rolling backward in that brakeless car down a steep hill. It's time to quit settling for crumbs. Time for your mantra to be, "show me the whole pie."

You've learned well with your family not to give away your truth in exchange for love, but with other people you give yourself away all the time. You want to please the captain. You want to please the crew. It's disturbing for me to hear about because it's an echo of past neediness. Jeanne still trying to please the man in charge. This is once again about the pain you're in, the pain you're not admitting to anyone, not even yourself. It's about your hands. You're trying so hard to be accepted and liked, but what will it mean if you destroy yourself physically? I know this is a tough one to see because you're smack in the middle of it, but promise me you'll spend some time thinking about what you really need and where you're going.

I hope we can talk on the phone after you get this letter. I hear your argument now: "But Elizabeth, I have always taken risks and sought adventures. I have always wanted to go to sea. Anyway, I need the job. I need the money." That's all true, but more than anything else, you need yourself, intact.

Paul and I send our love,

Elizabeth

I turn off the light over my bunk but can't sleep. It's an ache from inside that starts at my elbows and travels down to my fingertips. For several weeks it's been only my left hand, but this week it's my right hand too. When I'm asleep, the bottom thumb knuckle of my right hand turns backward like it's broken, and if I touch it, it's excruciatingly painful. If I gently pull the joint forward with my left hand, it snaps back into place.

Trying to get my mind to stop dwelling on the pain, I lie thinking of past joys, of the many things I miss: my house, art on the walls, a queen sized bed, my yard, flowers butterflies and colorful birds; my daughters, my friends, Elizabeth and Paul; dancing in softly lit rooms, writing at my comfortable desk, green grass, sitting in quiet sunshine, reading for long stretches of time; doing absolutely nothing; painting rich, thick oil paints onto a canvas with a palette knife. With all these things running in my head I doze off and fall into a deep sleep.

Chapter Eleven

Sergei

Once again I marvel at the natural beauty of Valdez. I know that you don't always view the beauty of nature that surrounds you, but something keeps drawing my eye to this place. Something strikes a chord inside me and I don't know if it is the white snow and glaciers, the deep blue of the sea, the dark green of the lush forests or the way the sun shines down on everything. Maybe it is just the combination of it all or maybe it is just the difference of splendor between Valdez and the various places where I have lived my life. The scenery in Valdez is always breathtaking as if you are seeing it for the first time though it may be the hundredth. Add the fact that adorable animals are always somewhere to be found, and no one can reject the idea that Valdez is a real life masterpiece.

Before breakfast I take an opportunity to revel in this city's beauty while stopping on the deck to gather myself. While on the deck I hear a small splash off to my left and see three small otters swimming in the vicinity. Two are floating on their backs while the other bobs in the water watching them. I find it funny how at ease the otters are as they rest on their backs. They appear as happy as can be as with their little hind feet stretched into the air. They fare much better swimming on their back than I usually do; even when they enter the choppy wake of a crossing boat. Even when some water splashes over one of the otter's faces, he continues to swim relaxed on his back. No choking on the water for him.

Scruggs gets off the ship after breakfast in Valdez. He leaves with a smile on his face and a slightly thinner wallet. I feel dwarfed as Dave, the new cook, towers over me and hands me three twenty-dollar bills as we leave port. He's in a great mood.

"Scruggs asked me to give you this," Dave nods.

"Sixty bucks?"

"That's about right. A dollar a day," he says.

"I haven't been tipped since my second week on board, when Pete got off. Left me twenty bucks in his room."

He looks annoyed. "Al never gave you tips from the officers when they left the ship?" Dave asks.

"No."

"Doesn't surprise me. Nothing surprises me about Al."

Suddenly I remember the times Rich commented on the generosity of the officers and wonder why I didn't put two and two together.

"Jeanne, these guys always, and I mean always, leave generous tips. They give them to the cook, who in turn gives them to the steward assistant."

I remember the time the first engineer handed a wad of bills to Al, then looked in my direction.

"So, Al pocketed my tips?"

"Sorry. I'm really sorry you had to work with him. He's the only cook I know who would do that," Dave shakes his head.

On the stern, I bid an early farewell to the waterfalls tucked into the rocks, the eagles and cormorants soaring above and the otters and seals in the bay. I think about what Elizabeth said in her letter, how I've been grateful for crumbs. But the fact that the fat-assed, lazy slob had the audacity to steal my hard-earned tips, makes me red-hot mad. I'd like to ring his thick neck.

I go into Valdez this morning with Vanessa. While she's at the bank and making phone calls, I order a Mocha Latte and a raspberry-filled pastry in a café. The place is busy with its breakfast crowd but I'm able to find a small table where I sit and leisurely read a magazine; imagine that, leisurely doing anything! Vanessa joins me for the short half an hour before she has to return to the ship. She bitches the entire time. I don't mind; I know she needs to do this. I know I'm the only safe person with whom she can talk. It's just that I want to stay positive until I get off the ship. When her cab pulls up, we hug and kiss through her tears.

After Vanessa leaves, I walk in the freezing rain to a chiropractor's office to see if I can get an adjustment and possibly a massage; unfortunately, they're closed today. The woman in the shop next door calls all the massage therapists in town for me, but no luck.

I'm drenched when I return to the café. The bustling breakfast place has changed into a quiet, empty room. I order decaffeinated tea and a piece of homemade Baklava. I savor each sip, each bite, each moment I am able to relax outside of the O.S. Illinois. The waiter, Tom, says it's fine for me to read my magazine and stay as long as I want.

Tom's a red-haired Irish man who moved here on whim. He always loved cold weather and heard that it was gorgeous up here. He informs me he doesn't plan on ever leaving. He loves the cold, the scenic mountains and the freedom. I envy him for doing what he wants—moving to Alaska and just trying it out. Then I realize, I am following my dreams too. I am working hard, but I am making money and living my dream. How many teachers can say they have ever been out to sea for over a day? I return to the ship in time to set up for lunch.

This afternoon we disembark from Valdez and once again head south. Ironic that as we leave the Valdez Channel behind and the coastal mountains recede to a mist, my view contracts.

The ship, fully loaded with oil, rides low in the water. So low that, standing amidships, I could make a comfortable if scary high dive into the sea. Twenty feet. *Bye-bye Jeanne.*

I glance back toward the coast. Smudge of mountains, pale sky above. It could be any dime-store painting hung over a plaid couch: a perspective we are used to, which triggers that comfortable feeling about nature's open spaces. Not so on the sea.

Looking forward I see there is no horizon so close as on the open sea. Without land, with no points of reference at all, and only twenty feet of elevation between me and the water, I might as well be standing on a ladder in a cornfield in central Kansas. And when the sea is still like this and I keep me gaze oceanward, I cannot even tell we're moving.

With me thumb and forefinger I create a viewfinder. Sometimes reducing the world to its minimums enlarges what you see. As I look through it, the sea suddenly changes. I'm lost in grey and white tumbling water when the ship's whistle blasts.

It blasts again.

Whales starboard. A pod of giant black and white killer whales races alongside us. Fast and graceful, they split the waves and criss-cross each other's paths.

Dave and Rich come flying down the back steps from the galley to see what is happening. ABs line up along the bridge wing. It seems the entire crew is on deck for the play, the sport, the belly-flopping orcas. Figarino blasts the horn one last time, and we all cheer.

Later in the evening I take my usual walk, this time with Vanessa. "Believe me, Jeanne, if I can handle being aboard this ship for sixty days, I can handle anything," she says. "I swear to God, you should feel the same way too. Two or three people would be doing the work you're doing on other ships."

"Out of the five ships you've been on, is this your most difficult voyage?" I ask.

"Definitely."

"Lucky us. Being here then."

"I keep telling you, we need to go on a luxury ship together. This tub is as old as any company allows their ships to get before they scrap them," she says. "At the end of the year it goes in for restoration to the tune of millions of dollars. Three years down the road, they'll scrap her. All that money invested for three short years—and they can't find you a dishwasher."

I bump into Rich that night in the passageway just before I head off to bed. We talk for a few minutes and I tell him what Vanessa told me earlier in the evening. He confirms some of Vanessa's claims and tells me, "New ships go across the sea by remote control. Due to the new technology on these ships, jobs are dwindling. Only two-hundred-fifty ships are currently union manned compared to twenty years ago when there were nine hundred. Those two-hundred-fifty ships haul ten times the cargo that nine hundred ships hauled twenty years ago. So everybody works longer, harder hours." Corporate greed. That's why my hands are aching.

Another week and we're in Long Beach Harbor. This time, though, we're at the dock, which means I don't have to climb down a rope ladder.

During my afternoon break I call for a cab. When it pulls up to the dock, Robby gets out and hands the driver two twenties. A bright pink bandanna covers his shiny black hair.

"For my fare and hers, too. Take her wherever she wants to go. Bring her back safely," he says all cool like to the cab driver, then nods at me like an older brother.

I protest needlessly. There's no outdoing Robby.

The cab driver is from Nigeria. He has been a United States resident for seven years, and when he finds out what I'm doing on the ship, he thinks I'm ridiculous.

"Don't do that work. You have education. Go back to teaching college," he says, looking back at me in his rearview mirror. "Why are you on a ship with a bunch of men with no education, using four letter words all the time?"

I try to assure him that isn't necessarily the case, but by the time we reach downtown Long Beach, I walk from the cab feeling depressed, having momentarily lost the vision of why I'm shipping. The cabby was well-intended, but sometimes even a sensitive person can misunderstand another's dreams.

I buy a five-dollar Quick Pick Lotto ticket for Rich and return to the waterfront where I listen to a Dixieland band. It's hot, almost ninety degrees. I sit in the sun. The jazz makes me feel almost spiritual. The sunshine's warmth on my face and body soothes me and seems to cure all my aches and pains. When the concert concludes I return to the ship to complete my afternoon tasks.

Before dinner, I round the corner to the crew mess and almost crash into Rich. He looks pale, almost as if he's scared. Maybe it's the flu.

"New dishwasher delivered this afternoon," he says. "Couple of engineers installed it, but guess what?"

"Do I want to know?"

"They finally got it hooked up, but, well, it's a land-going machine. Not a sea-going machine."

"Tell me you're joking."

"No, ma'am. Bunch of sorry dill weeds, if you ask me. They're sending it back."

I leave before he sees me fall apart.

Later Figarino catches me off guard at the chow line waiting for dinner.

"How's your job going, Jeanne? Doing okay with everything?"

I think about what Elizabeth said about pleasing the man in charge, take a deep breath. "Sir, there's the matter of the broken dishwasher that's been inoperable since I got on. The way I have to sterilize the dishes is really taking its toll on my hands."

Rich nods, then nods some more while he putzes with his salad bar.

"I thought we had the dishwasher problem solved a long time ago. No one informed me that the darned new machine we picked up didn't work." He's on fire.

Disheartened, after supper duties are completed, I return to my room and take a nap. I awake refreshed and ready to dance off the disappointment. Come hell, come high water, I am going ashore tonight for a good evening out on the town. I take some time to get myself ready. Which pair of jeans will look just right, the blue or the black? I find the perfect top and put on makeup. I adjust my scarf, fluff my hair, fling a sultry look at the mirror and head out.

As if on cue, a taxi is waiting for me when I walk off the ship. I have it drop me off at a seafood restaurant that comes highly recommended. I eat oysters on the half shell, Caesar salad and a piece of key lime pie. Again, it feels sublime to be waited on and eat without rushing. I leave a gargantuan tip.

Next I hit a blues cafe where I sit at the only empty seat at the bar next to a guy with long dark hair and a lined face. He drinks black coffee and wears an outdated polyester beige suit with a big, pointed collar. He reeks of the worst smelling after-shave, ever. Other than that, he's somewhat attractive. He tells me he is a guitarist and singer. We talk about our heroes: Clapton, Carole King, James Brown, Aretha, Janis, Stevie Ray. Then about him never getting married and about me being married to my opposite. He's intrigued by my tenacity.

"Hats off to you," he says when I tell details of tanker hell.

The band starts up. "It's time for me to dance now," I say, having explained earlier that I'd be up and dancing when the music started.

Without hesitating I get out there; I'm the first person on the floor. Dancing by myself, I execute a few fancy moves to the first three fast songs and when a slow, Chicago blues song starts, I continue dancing. Someone taps me on my shoulder.

A Russian accent says, "Come on. Please. Now you dance with me."

During the dance, Sergei begins selling himself to me, explaining that he is a crazy, fun-loving, Russian sailor who works on a yacht in the harbor. The slow song ends. A fast one begins.

Sergei is, without a doubt, the most uninhibited dancer I've ever partnered with. The wilder he gets, the crazier

I become. He struts like a rooster with his elbows behind his back. He gets low to the ground and moves his elbows up and down while he makes funny faces. He shimmies. He turns his back and we dance back-to-back. Other dancers clear a space for us. We're good. Really good.

A short while later his two Russian friends show up, and from time to time he talks with them briefly while I keep right on dancing. I'm thinking I could be attracted to a man like Sergei. In these exuberant moments, anyway, I believe I could love a man like Sergei. Wild. Crazy. Spontaneous. All the things I usually am not but sometimes madly desire. But when he slides his hand down onto my lower back, I remove it and place it up on the small of my back. A couple of times he tries to dance with both hands wrapped around my waist. I don't let them stay that way for more than a few seconds.

When the band stops, so do we. We sit outside. I sip red wine while Sergei guzzles beer. "What I really like to drink is wadka. I really like wadka," he says straight-faced. "Wadka. Yummm."

He pours part of his beer into my empty wine glass, talks about a beer drinking contest where you can't use your hands to pick up the glass. He leans forward, picks up my glass in his teeth, drinks the beer with no hands. I laugh, then laugh some more.

I can't explain our connection. Even with the language barrier, we still have great conversations about Russian versus American politics, shipping, world cuisine. We make each other laugh. In no time we're up dancing again. Showcasing dips, intricate whirls and steps I never thought I knew, we feed off the other's zaniness.

Sergei isn't handsome by American standards. However, perfect features have never appealed to me. His buddies are much more the macho, full-chested kind of guys. Sergei has high cheek bones, a wide face across the eyes, a straight nose and semi-full lips. He's also thin and very athletic. I'm extremely thin now, too. Periodically both of us stop on the dance floor to pull up our jeans. The band takes its second break and we sit down.

After a few minutes of idle chitchat, Sergei turns to me and says, "Jeanne. Vat you vant to do? You vant to dance, you vant to drink, you vant to…?" Sergei raises his eyebrows, smiles.

If an American guy said that to me in the same situation, I'd tell him to take a flying leap. But with Sergei, I laugh. I see the band members taking their positions on stage once more. "Sergei, I vant to dance," I say and lead him back onto the dance floor.

During the last set we relax with each other. Now I like him so much that I raise both hands up and wrap them around his neck. He looks like a dog that just swallowed a bone.

The last set ends. "I need to call a cab," I say.

"I'll come with you," he says.

I ignore his offer as I try to gather my thoughts. "Excuse me for just a few moments while I go to the ladies room."

Sergei's waiting on the Victorian sofa behind the pool tables when I walk out of the ladies room. He pats the cushion beside him.

"Jeanne. Come sit beside me, now please. Come on. Come here now."

Unable to resist, I walk over and sit beside him.

"Jeanne. We have danced. We have drank. We can't go to my ship. We can't go to your ship. We get a hotel until you go back to work in the morning."

I just look into his eyes sadly. "I can't do that."

"Why? Why can we not do that? Why Jeanne? I like you. And Jeanne, I know you like me too. Don't you?"

I nod my head yes.

"So why not?" He looks at me like a child asking for truth.

I forget every sensible reason why not; I forget that he could be a would-be ax-murderer, have AIDS or be married with ten kids. Despite this, I can't forget my own inner restraints or perhaps it is my ultimate desire for a true lasting love and not a one-night stand.

"Because Sergei, I just can't. That's all I know."

"I know you want to, don't you?"

Again, I nod my head yes.

"Then we get hotel and for this one night, you be my woman."

Playfully, he pulls me to him, chest to chest. "And now, you must kiss me."

We roll until my back's pressed into the cushion. He kisses me.

It's like no other kiss I've had in my life. He nibbles my lips, my tongue and the inside of my mouth. He gently rests one hand on my breast, the other on my thigh. I'm drowning in his kiss. It makes me give in. The kiss lasts two, maybe three minutes. I want to go to a hotel with him but still I can't. The time? Work the next day? No. Fear of losing my heart? Reluctantly, I end the kiss.

"Now Jeanne, we go to the hotel. Yes?"

"No, Sergei. Now I go to my ship."

"But why Jeanne? Why? I like you. You like me. Why not? Tell me please. Tell me why not."

"I wish I could Sergei, but I just can't." He follows me out to the sidewalk where we wait for my taxi, arm-in-arm. The driver opens the back door, Sergei kisses me one last time, softly, good-bye. I watch his sad face as the cab pulls away. Watch as he sits on the curb, resting his head on his folded arms.

Chapter Twelve

Fairy Tales

The days between Long Beach and Valdez stretch on and on, seemingly forever. I've sailed this route before and am tired of my routine. I continue on though. Lots of the guys are coming down with a flu bug. Perhaps I have a touch of it; maybe that's why I feel so listless. I amuse myself by watching videos on the small television and VCR set up in my room. I choose comedies from the crew lounge video assortment. They make me laugh and forget about how I feel. It takes several days to finish one, because twenty minutes into a movie, I always fall fast asleep.

Vanessa drops by during the short half hour we have to talk before her shift starts.

"Come in," I say, opening my door. "Boy, do I need to talk with you."

I tell her about my evening with Sergei, about the long, passionate kiss and wanting to make love with a total stranger.

"Don't worry about not fulfilling that desire, Jeanne. I've done it and the reality is never as good as the dream." She glances at her watch, realizes its time for her to report to her post, and gives me a quick hug before running down to the engine room.

Once again, I'm left to my solitude. I generally enjoy being alone. I'm pretty good company, but sometimes I long to share my life with someone I truly love who loves me in return and with whom I can build a future. I miss holding, being held. Maybe that's what my attraction to Sergei was all about: loneliness. It was similar to when I ran away from home at seventeen and kissed a sailor on the train ride from my parent's house in Georgia to my sister's home in Illinois. Two lonely people gravitating to each other for kindness, comfort, touch. Something that feels like love at the moment but isn't the real thing.

I decide to go down and get some fresh air. The sun is taking a break. Everything's gray. Gray sea, gray sky, gray thoughts. Even the dingy green walls and decks look gray. I think the monotony of sea life's getting to me, but when I come upon a few crew members minutes later, I begin to think monotony is not so bad. Having a schedule can be a good thing. Besides, the pattern I have on the ship is much better than what I had on land in my last job.

Everyone's talking about storms. The season for storms is apparently at hand. The mates talk about the big storms they've been in as if they stayed cool and collected all the way through. Don't know if I believe that. They say that if we really get nailed, a storm could rock us for five or six days. It's more frequent to hit nasty weather up north in the gulf of Alaska, but the entire coast is treacherous this time of year with its coastal storm patterns and wave systems that make a ship roll side-to-side.

"Stanley," I ask after listening to them for a while, "with all the sophisticated weather equipment, why would a ship knowingly go into a storm? If we know we're headed into one, why don't we just turn around?"

"Well kiddo, we're balancing money, time and safety—in that order. Schedule gets top billing. If we get behind, we lose money. Planes can carry air cargo above storm clouds, but they can't haul even a small portion of what's transported on container ships, so we're a vital part of world trade. Still, we have to do it quickly and cheaply or risk being labeled obsolete." Stanley's bald head wrinkles.

"So, it may be safer to head away from a storm, but we don't?"

"Not unless it's unusually bad, and sometimes that's

impossible to know until you're in it." Now my brows are so furrowed they are probably touching each other. Stanley tries to cheer me. "Jeanne, do you know the difference between a fairy tale and a sea story?"

"No."

"Well, a fairy tale begins with, 'Once upon a time' and a sea story begins with, 'This ain't no shit.'" He has a little smirk on his face as he continues, "A fairy tale ends with, 'And they all lived happily ever after,' while a sea story ends with, 'And ever since then everything's been fucked up.'"

"Geez, Stanley. Surrounded by so much comfort and reassurances, what's a girl to say?"

We're one day away from Valdez and things are piling up. It's hectic. Schedules are shot to hell because of surprise boat and fire drills—all on linen change day. What a frickin' nightmare. Everyone's pissed.

During the drill we're on the upper deck checking our gear when Kyle walks over to tell Vanessa and me, "In an emergency we don't use the life boats. They're slow and ineffective. Instead, try to get on one of the rafts stored in the forecastle."

I take a deep breath and try not to panic as I wonder why he is telling us this.

Rich is cranky. For one thing, he usually makes his salads in the morning: three bean, shrimp, tuna, coleslaw, melon, cucumber and tomato. His face turns bright red with anger at the safety meeting when the new second mate asks about safety concerns.

"Yeah. I got a safety concern," Rich says. "It's called canned soup for lunch. No time to make anything else. And as far as the broken dishwasher goes, I'm still carrying scalding hot water to the sink. Jeanne's still using tongs."

The second mate writes down Rich's complaint. Big whoop. As if that will fix anything.

"Everyone's in a bad mood, huh?" Kyle leans over and whispers.

I reply, "Yeah, in a big way."

Kyle sees the bird before I do. "Look, an albatross," he whispers, not wanting to disrupt the meeting. But the bird has a different idea. Suddenly, it's dive-bombing Kyle's head.

Arms waving, Kyle curses then cries out, "Geez, take it easy, pal!"

Robby and I burst into fits of laughter and the bird backs off. The second mate is not impressed with our antics.

"Have you ever read *The Rhyme of the Ancient Mariner?*" Kyle asks.

"Of course—great poem. Do you think that bird will follow the ship like the one in Colridge's poem?"

Stanley, who must have overheard my question, shouts, "Oh my God! Gag her quick, Kyle. Rich, don't be surprised if all the food in the cooler goes bad."

Rich busts a gut laughing at Stanley's comment.

Stanley approaches me with a look of mock-horror on his face and asks me in a Boris Karloff voice, "Haven't you ever read the end of *The Rhyme of the Ancient Mariner?*" He looks left, then right and whispers in my ear, "Don't you know the bad luck it can bring to talk about... *that bird following us?*"

The drills put me way behind on cleaning the rooms. I'm in a cleaning locker on D Deck rinsing a mop with the storm talk rummaging about in the back of my mind when I think about my daughters and how much I miss them. I wonder how they're doing, when I'll see them again. I think about how they're the best gifts I've ever received, how they've taught me more about love than any other life experience. Suddenly, there, in the cramped, dingy cleaning closet, I lean against the wall, slide down and sit, resting my head against the trash can.

Exhausted and feeling like a cold is coming on I write a list to keep me going.

Things that energize my spirit:
1. *Yoga. I do yoga almost every day now while the guys take their 10:00 A.M. coffee break.*
2. *Walking in the fresh air with the wind blowing and the sea changing color.*
3. *Meditating, especially when the weather's good and I hide behind that white box on the bow where no one can see me, even from the bridge.*

4. *Writing to friends and loved ones.*
5. *Vanessa. Having her here is a blessing.*

Then I write a poem:

Never
If I never see a mop again
it will be all right
or a water pitcher, margarine
tub or coffee maker for twenty
I'd be happy...or
floor stripper, or toilet bowl or even a dirty
mirror—their absence would delight
my soul.

We're in and out of Valdez faster than ever. No turnaround time whatsoever. I catch a cold and my first day back on my feet Kyle and I are standing outside on the stern clinging tightly to the handholds on the side of the house when I catch a glimpse of wistfulness in his eyes.

"What drew you to the sea?" I ask.

He looks out at the ocean sort of mystically. "I've always loved being out here. Sunrises and sunsets, clearest skies you've ever seen, all the stars."

"Yeah. I've seen a few of those and they're intoxicating."

"Working at sea is like nothing else. Constant busy-ness, working seven days a week, manning watches. Granted, it's stressful, but for me it's an opportunity to do what I really want. Work with my hands at something I love. Engineering. And in a place I love."

He looks at me to see if I get it.

I nod.

"For me it's not only a way to make money, it's a way of life," he adds.

For him it's adventure. Travel. A chance to see far off parts of the world and experience strange and exotic things most people never know.

"It's not all the beautiful sunrises and sunsets though, even for experienced sailors there are frightening moments," he admits.

"I hear you."

Tonight the sea looks like a lake. No waves. Not even a ripple. A golden sun sets against dark purple puff clouds.

Staring at the sky, Kyle takes a deep breath. "Trouble's brewing," he says quietly.

"Yeah, I think you're right," I respond.

I go back to my room, his words spinning in my head. My throat is scratchy, my nose is stuffed. I can't sleep. Finally I decide to write Elizabeth and Paul to try to work out the tension I'm beginning to feel creeping in the air.

Dear Paul and Elizabeth,

What a day. What a week. I got into a bit of trouble with my buddies, Kyle and Robby, at the last safety meeting. It all started with an albatross trying to fly into Kyle's head. He was flailing his arms and cursing and Robby and I couldn't help but laugh. The second mate looked annoyed at us during the meeting but didn't say much. Kyle told me later that after the meeting the second mate lit into him like nobody's business. Said it was no way for an officer to behave, stuff like that. Now Robby and I feel kind of bad about it because we didn't catch any flack. I guess that's one of the benefits of not being an officer, eh?

There's been a wretched cold/flu bug going around the ship. I haven't been feeling well for the past few days so I've been spending a lot of my free time lying in bed watching movies. The second engineer sold me his TV/VCR combo for fifty bucks when he got off. The crew lounge is filled with videos, a pretty good assortment, but the officers' lounge has an even better selection. I watch comedies that make me laugh and forget about how wretched I feel. But about twenty minutes into the movie, I fall fast asleep, so it takes me awhile to finish one.

Tonight I felt a little better and went up on the deck. The sky was so gray and ominous. The guys are saying that a storm's on the way. If we really get nailed, we could be stuck in the storm for five or six days. Ugh! We've already been caught in coastal storm patterns with wave systems that make us roll a lot—side to side—but apparently, they were nothing. The guys talk about the really big storms they've been in. They all say they stayed cool and collected all the way through—don't know if I believe that!

  Love you, miss you, can't wait to see your smiling faces.
Jeanne

  P.S. Do you know the difference between a fairy tale and a sea story?

  A fairy tale begins with, "Once upon a time."

  A sea story begins with, "This ain't no shit."

  A fairy tale ends with, "And they all lived happily ever after."

  A sea story ends with, "And ever since then everything's been fucked up."

Chapter Thirteen

Rough Seas

The storm blows in too soon. Unpredictable weather. Turbulent waters. Last night before I went to sleep, I leaned my body on the railing and gazed out onto the ocean, admiring its tranquility. It's my last week at sea, but there was no one tell except the moon and the stars.

In the middle of the night things started changing. In the morning, the ship is bouncing around to the rocking and rolling of the sea. Everyone's bitchy, especially the captain. At breakfast I'm hunched over the sink washing dishes when Figarino puts his arm through the pass-through window, slams an empty salt shaker down on the counter and walks away in a huff.

"That's sort of a command to fill it up and take it back in there with egg on your face," Rich says. Obviously neither the Captain, nor Rich know what kind of mood I'm in.

"Let's get this straight," I counter. "The officers' mess has four, count them, four salt and pepper shakers, two of which are on the table. It's reasonable to assume that the captain has a salt shaker within his reach. He sure as hell doesn't need to make an issue out of one of them being empty, especially given the fact I spent half my day yesterday in drills and safety meetings and had no time to do my job. If I walk in there this pissed off, I'll make a scene. Is that what you want me to do?"

"Well, I guess not. If you're that upset, you probably shouldn't go in there right now," Rich says. He's never seen me like this. He scratches the back of his head, looks perplexed. "Well now, never get in the path of a hot tempered woman, no sir. Not my wife. Not Jeanne either. No siree."

He knows I hear him. He's smiling and both eyebrows are scrunched into a fake frown. Finally, I laugh. But I don't take the salt shaker to Figarino.

I'm eerily fascinated by the giant waves. I watch the angry sea whipping up a frenzy and remember the time my oldest daughter Emily was six months old and we were vacationing in the Gulf of Mexico when a big storm like this hit. Just as today, the storm was brewing. The surf was up.

My mother-in-law watched my six-month-old daughter in the motel room while my husband and I rode the waves on air mattresses. Close by, a stranger did the same thing. We caught several strong waves that crashed us onto the beach. Then the three of us went out again, smiling and laughing.

None of us expected anything to happen, but suddenly we were swept far out into the Gulf. I watched as our motel became a small white dot on the horizon. All I could think about was Emily and how I wanted to live so I could raise her. The waves got rougher and criss-crossed between the three of us. The last thing I saw before the rogue wave tore the air mattress out from under me was the look of terror on my husband's face.

I came up sputtering, felt my legs being sucked down toward the ocean's bottom. Barely able to keep my head above water, I prayed. Actually, I bargained with God.

"Look, I know I'm no better than anyone else in this world, but I'm my baby's mom and she's so little and I

love her more than anything. Please let me live and get back to shore so I can be her mom. Please God, help me."

Just then the stranger called to me in Spanish. "Aqui! Over here!"

There he was about twenty feet away, still on his air mattress, one arm outstretched to me. His face looked determined. Using every bit of strength I had, I tried to swim toward him, but the sea kept moving me further away.

"Come on. You can do it!" he yelled.

And then, as if my prayers were being answered, a big zig zag wave pushed me directly into him. He held me as close as a mother holds her child.

The surge of water that pushed the three of us back to shore came as unexpectedly as the one that had taken us out. Before we knew what was happening, the stranger and I were dumped onto the shore about a mile down the beach from the motel. We crawled onto the beach where I saw Kirby and his air mattress roll in, and for what seemed like forever, the three of us collapsed on the warm sand, struggling to regain our strength. I said another prayer. This time a thank you.

When I opened my eyes, the stranger was kneeling over my face asking if I was okay. I sat up to thank him, asked what I could do to repay him. But he just smiled,

shook his head and looked into my eyes one last time
before he turned and slowly walked away.

It's a humbling experience to have your life saved by
a total stranger. Humbling and moving. Ever since then I've
been asking what I'm supposed to be doing with this life of
mine that's been spared from drowning twice, both times by
strangers.

At lunchtime the rollers make the galley sway so much that
Dave and Rich and I can't avoid bumping into each other. I lift
some trays, the floor tilts and Rich and I are butt to butt. We
can't help but laugh.

To divert everyone's mind from the storm Dave puts
on a fast food, high caloric, high fat, American lunch of ham-
burgers, French fries and milkshakes. It's a hit! We have them
coming back for thirds. Big Dave's in heaven. He even takes
the time to put a pat of butter on the buns and lightly toast
them before serving the burgers.

"Hey. Could I have a plain bun Dave?" Todd, the diabetic, asks from the chow line. He's lifting up his bun, making a face.

"You mean not toasted?" Dave asks.

"No, toasted's okay. I mean no butter. It's the cholesterol."

With his back turned to the chow line, Dave whispers to me, "The guy has to watch his sugar intake and has high cholesterol. He orders a double cheeseburger with fries but doesn't want butter on the bun. Is he for real?"

I crack up and just when I calm down a little, Dave adds, "And a milkshake."

We laugh so hard that Figarino comes into the galley and asks if we're okay. I look at his grim face and realize it must be hard to laugh in troubled seas when you're the one in command.

The wind's blowing so hard by the afternoon that Vanessa and I have to hold on to each other to keep from falling down as we walk along the deck.

This 100,000 ton, dead-weight steel tanker shudders, shakes and creaks. At the end of one long roll, I hear a horrendous "snap." I feel the entire ship shake from bow to stern, groaning and rumbling, like it's going to come apart and, at the same time, I feel like I'm going to come apart too. But when you're out in the middle of it, you do what you need to do and count on each other. We're all we've got. I have faith in Vanessa and Kyle and Scruggs. I trust the deckhands to come through. And even though Figarino is feeling the strain, I am confident in his abilities. It's the O.S. Illinois that stops my heart.

"Jeanne, try to think about getting to port," Vanessa says, her arm laced through mine as we slip and slide on the stern. I look up at the waves above our head, all perspective lost now that we're surrounded by a circle of swells which leave only a tiny dome of sky above our heads. How strange to be on this vast body of water that suddenly looks so small and feels so claustrophobic.

Soon the decks are closed. We're locked inside the house.

If the weather were normal, it would take us four days to get from Valdez to Bellingham, but as the storm intensifies, Rich says, "We'll get there when we get there. Kind of like road trips when your kids were little. Nothing to worry about. This ship's been through lots of autumn storms up and down this coast."

Practical jokes are suddenly the "in" thing. The crew is acting like a bunch of school kids playing pranks on each other, escapades. I can tell they need to talk and so I listen to their jokes even if I've heard them before. Stanley tells a story about a new deck hand that came on many years ago with no experience whatsoever.

"The first mate told the guy that he had the mail buoy watch and sent him out to the bow with a whistle and a set of binoculars. It was cold outside, very cold, but they made him stand out on the bow of the ship with instructions to blow the whistle when he spotted the mail buoy. Of course, there's no such thing as a mail buoy, but they kept him out there for an hour until finally, the first mate said, 'That's enough. Bring him in.' The deck hand was an ice cube when he came in and saw all the guys busting their guts laughing." It's all about tradition, rites of passage.

Robby says one time his crew got together and took pictures of big muscle-bound guys from workout magazines and pasted photos of their own heads onto the hard, chiseled bodies. Then they took a picture of a baby and pasted the first mate's photo onto the soft, round body. The caption read, *We're gonna have fun in the storm.* They made copies and put them on all the ship's bulletin boards. The first mate knew who did it, but he let it slide. All he said was to take them down. No one was reprimanded.

At dinner Rich decides we need to play a joke on the captain to lessen the tension. He starts teasing me. "You know how you and the captain share the same addiction to chocolate syrup on ice cream? Well, I got an idea," he says. "You take that menu up to the bridge and when you get back down here, I'll tell you what it is."

I go up and the captain orders his usual: a serving of rice, tuna salad and butter. He doesn't say butter, he just writes it on the menu.

Rich reads the captain's order sporting a wide grin as he plunks down a brand new jar of chocolate syrup on the tray beside the tuna and rice.

"No way. I'm not taking that chocolate syrup up there." I shake my head.

"Come on. We gotta see if the old man's sense of humor is intact."

I keep shaking my head no.

"Okay, I'll take the rap," Rich says. "But don't say anything to him unless he says something. Then just tell him it was all my idea."

I know that Figarino needs an outlet for the anxiety, and so I reluctantly agree. I take up the tray with the rice, tuna and a plastic squeeze jar of Hershey's syrup. At this point, however, neither of us realize that we've omitted a most important ingredient: butter. The captain must have butter for his rice. Luckily, Figarino is on the far side of the bridge when I hand the tray to the AB who answers the door.

"He didn't even see the chocolate?" Rich asks when I get back down to the galley.

"Nope," I say.

"Well, we should be getting a phone call real soon," Rich says.

Just then the phone rings. Rich's face looks grim while he listens. After a few minutes, he hangs up and turns to me.

"That was Donny calling to say the captain wants his butter. We forgot the damned butter."

I grab the butter and run for the stairwell. Run is a misnomer. I move as fast as I can up four flights for the third time on a ship that is rocking and rolling. I'm greeted at the door by a scowling Figarino, chocolate syrup in hand.

"You want to take the Hershey's syrup down with you?" he asks.

"Sir, the chocolate was from the steward, especially for you." I hand him the butter.

"So the chocolate was on purpose?"

"Sir, the steward thought you might need it for strength during the rough seas."

I peer out the windows of the bridge and my eyes grow wide as a wall of water rises up over the bow and crashes over the length of the ship's deck. This, Hershey's chocolate syrup cannot fix.

Figarino sees me tremble and explains, "That's thirty feet of solid water. When the mass of our bow goes down into one of these, instead of spray and foam coming up over the bow, it's solid water like a brick wall. Green water, we call it. It's the sheer force that can rip off mooring winches and anchor windlasses. Just be glad you're on a wide tanker and not a long, narrow Navy ship. We'd be rolling even more."

He shows me an instrument that looks like a carpenter's level with a bubble, only it's bowed instead of straight. I think he calls it an inclinometer. There are two of them. One runs vertical to measure the intensity of the pitch, the other horizontal to measure the roll.

"The red lines are danger zones. They let us know when it's really bad. Some captains turn tail and run as fast as they can to get out of a storm when the pitch and roll get too intense," he says as he looks me dead in the eyes. "But don't worry, I am not one of those."

Phew! I think, relieved to learn our captain isn't afraid to sail us directly into a dangerous storm with no thought of turning back.

One of the mates interrupts my anxious thoughts. "Wind's gusting at eighty knots, sir."

Figarino turns away from me and walks toward windows facing the bow, but as he does I glimpse a smile that turns up the corners of his mouth.

When I tell Rich, he stomps his foot. "Gotta make him laugh in times like these or he'll have a heart attack or something worse from the stress," Rich says.

"I couldn't sleep if I had Figarino's job. Storm or no storm," I sigh.

Later Kyle plays devil's advocate when I tell him about the chocolate incident. "Okay, here you are. The ship is its own island, and there you are in charge, carrying hundreds of thousands of tons of oil. It's a potential disaster waiting to happen, and you're the captain up on the bridge. Underneath you are all of your crew members. Thirty people or more. And one of the things that begins to happen is that people begin to get familiar, cozy and comfortable, and the next thing you know, somebody's not looking where they're supposed to be looking, and a storm like this one begins heating up. So from the captain's point of view, the chocolate represents something larger."

"Okay, the captain may be a bit of a martinet, but he is intelligent and has courage," I say, trying to keep the conversation going for a few more minutes and our minds off the storm.

"Well, I'm theorizing now, but part of the function of discipline is that you're dealing with people who, without it, may not be able to function in emergencies."

"So it's important to keep a tight rein," I say.

"Just between you and me, I expect that the way the captain talks to all of us is the way he talks to himself," Kyle says.

The gunmetal skies send wind and driving rain slamming against the portholes. The thirty-foot waves continue, and all the guys on board say they'll be getting bigger. Like the sea, the tension on the ship is mounting. I'm feeling it, too. I'm so nervous my hands are shaking. The old rust bucket is battered by another wave and it sounds like a car crash. There's no place to go where we can forget about the weather; it's at the center of every conversation on the ship. But no one's talking about being afraid. They just keep working and swapping storm stories.

As the sea pounds away, Rich says, "It's lucky for us we're loaded down with our cargo. Eighty percent of the ship that's under water isn't affected so much by the waves. If we were in ballast, lighter, sitting higher up with a higher center of gravity, we'd be rolling big time."

The decks are secured. No one's allowed outside, and we're really feeling the roll. Not to mention the claustrophobia. Now we're moving through turbulent water outside and inside the O.S. Illinois. Water spurts up from the galley sinks and there's flooding down in the engine room and steering gear room. Talk about wild seas.

I'm more tired by day three of rough seas than I can ever remember being in my life. It's hard to sleep. With all the extra effort required from my hands in the turbulence— holding tight to railings in the stairwells and passageways to stay balanced—my hands are screaming. But now my shoulders hurt too; shoulders, back, arms. I ache all over.

Walking toward my room, I see Robby who, like the others, wants to talk. Robby says, "Did you know the O.S. Illinois has been in dry dock to patch up holes in the steel hull caused from hitting the waves too hard and fast, to the tune of millions of dollars?"

This news does not comfort me, but I mumble, "It will be all right."

"Okay, landlubber," he says with a smile

"Good night," I reply wearily.

In my room, I begin to write a letter.

Dear Elizabeth & Paul,

We're in a monster storm. It's a big timer. The average swells are as high as a house. This ship which once seemed huge to me now feels like it doesn't weigh an ounce. We're getting thrown around like straws in the wind. Once in awhile we get hit by a bigger and nastier set of waves that changes the timing, and we get brutally tossed around.

My friends here keep telling me not to worry, because we can trust this ship. They know what this ship can do but I'm scared anyway. Scared and too damned tired to imagine seas worse than those we already face. I just keep telling myself we'll get through this, but I'm not sure I believe it.

Once I longed for adventure and now I am eager to find my way home.

Love,

Jeanne

Stuff is banging around all over the place. At the end of each hard roll I hear loud crashes in the room above, then more crashes that come roaring from other parts of the ship. It sounds like pieces of the hull are coming loose, and being tossed, helter-skelter.

It's amazing how people react to situations like this. In a weird sort of way, a big storm levels the playing field. We're all scared and want to live, so everyone does whatever they have to do to get stuff done. No one's strutting around barking orders. No one is pulling rank. It helps to infuse calm into an otherwise terrified heart. No one is thinking, *Oh well, we can just walk away from this.* The adrenaline kicks in, the rush is going and we're all thinking, *Okay—this is life or death*. And our ragged crew has turned into a team—one that is too feisty to let death win.

On my way down to the galley, the stairwell's a clogged artery with people running up and down. Robby passes me on his way down, taking five steps at a time, yelling, "Rich needs us in the mess halls. Flooding. Couple portholes out."

Two portholes are blown out by one of the big freak waves that pound the side of the ship. The water is thrown across the crew mess and smashes against the refrigerator. ABs patch up the openings with plywood, but the weak material keeps ripping apart. Robby and I mop the incoming water as fast as we can while Rich and Dave do the same in the galley. Robby is working harder and faster than anyone I've ever seen. We don't talk much, but occasionally he glances over at me as I struggle with a heavy bucket. In come three ABs to give us damage updates; that last set of high waves took out both lifeboats.

Chapter Fourteen

Taming the Wild Seas

The next two days we don't move. We're sitting in the storm, going slow ahead, hitting the big waves, and at this point I only know one thing for sure. There are as many different versions of the storm as there are people on the ship—it all depends on perspective, on where the person is when the shit hits the fan. The storm looks a hell of a lot different to the mates and ABs up on the bridge than it does to the QMEDs and engineers down in the hole or to us in the galley, for that matter.

Water is coming up over the bow and gushing back all the way to the bridge. The engineers are working around the clock to keep water out of the hole. Water is a constant in the galley. Trying to stay on our feet, we skate our way through it as pots and pans fly around. Robby tries to keep the passageways clear of debris while being tossed from one side to another. Many of the guys who've been making this run for over twenty years say the same thing: this is one of the worst storms they've ever seen.

Lunch starts with an easy menu, nothing homemade and nothing requiring sharp knives for chopping: canned tomato soup and fruit cocktail with grilled cheese sandwiches. The guys are lined up, trays in hand, going through the chow line teasing Rich and Dave about the prefab soup and salad, and I'm picking up pots and pans that have fallen from the rack when we hit the biggest roll yet. Food flies out of the serving bin. Rich and the guys in line are spattered with a mixture of red soup and chunky fruit. They look like they've been vomited on by a giant. Dave's standing at the sinks when the geysers hit.

"The unknown bubbling up from the drain," he shouts, a little too much like a horror film for my taste. The smell of the sink geysers clears the chow line in half a second. Those boys sprint out of there so fast they're gone before I can turn around. Meanwhile, the three of us slip around in the goop. It's everywhere—on the overhead and deck, in our hair and on our clothes.

Rich looks around the galley and says, "Jeanne, you done got yourself a big-assed storm. Yes siree. I'm callin' her Big-Assed Bertha. Never seen nothing like it in my life."

There's flooding fore and aft. From the galley, Rich is hollering loud enough for the entire ship to hear. Big Bertha this. Big Bertha that. Oh, Big Bertha you mother, you.

As we clean the galley, Rich says when there's an emergency, he puts aside all the things he doesn't like about some jerk, because if it's him that falls in the water, he sure as hell wants somebody to help rescue him. I've taken to doing the same, making every possible effort to not lock horns with anyone. There's nowhere to go with it.

Whether to scare or comfort themselves I'm not sure, but the guys keep telling me stories about other traumatic sea experiences. I'm still trying to lend a sympathetic ear and listen, but it is tough to hear about these frightening storm stories, even when my listening helps the person telling the story.

Now it's the third mate's turn. He corners me and starts bragging. "This storm is not as big as when I was on a ship four years ago, and the alarm went off at six in the morning. We discovered the ship's main diesel generator blew a line and released forty gallons of lube oil all over the main engine. Huge fire hazard! It was Sunday morning, just as we were getting ready to pull into port. It was awesome to see how fast everybody reacted, especially because everyone was torn from their sleep when it happened. Everyone ran to their station and was ready to go. The engineers got everything shut down right away and there was no fire…just a big mess. But here's the thing. We were in calm water, so shutting down the engines was fine. But if we had been in big seas like these, shutting down the engine could have been really, really bad."

After his story, I decide to steer clear of the bridge, and instead, search for Vanessa. I find her in her room, listening to music. She's the only person I can confide in. I tell her how scared I am.

"Don't worry, Jeanne," she says. "I've never been worried about being lost at sea, never been in a situation bad enough to where I was really frightened."

"But this ship is old and in need of repair," I say.

"Don't be nervous about what's happening on the ship. Think about getting home. Keep your hands busy on your job," she says. "The old ship will ride these swells and we'll be just fine."

I try to follow Vanessa's instructions to be calm and confident it's impossible as I'm tossed about. Solid walls of green water roll over the bow and flood the decks all the way to the bridge. That's longer than two football fields. The engineers talk about working around the clock to keep water out of the engine rooms. Rich jokes about the stinking geysers spewing out of sinks and the kitchen equipment flying around. Robby complains about trying to keep the catch-all passageways clear. And I confess to falling on my ass— repeatedly—while trying to make the beds.

The swells are close to forty feet now. Even Vanessa becomes quiet. I begin to understand the strong need for story-telling, the closeness one gets from sharing. I want to be with other people now, too.

I abandon my bunk and go down for a snack. On the walk to the galley I'm constantly forced to shift my weight as the ship sways to keep from falling. One second I'm leaning forward; the next second I'm leaning backward. Now I'm climbing up stairs without any effort whatsoever as the ship dips down into a roll. My feet feel like they aren't even attached to my body. The ship rolls from side-to-side. I'm using all my energy just to stay upright. It's exhausting. My elbows and knees become bruised as I'm thrown into bulkheads.

When I reach the mess halls they look as if they've been vandalized. Cracker baskets and fruit are strewn on the decks, chairs overturned, water fountain spewing. The windowless galley offers no point of reference; it's worse than looking out my porthole, which isn't great either because the view is either sky or water, depending on which side of the roll we're on. Two shades of gray, and that's all.

I abandon ideas of spending any time in the mess hall, wishing I could get some fresh air instead, but the decks are closed. That leaves the bridge. I remember that the captain told me to come up to the bridge whenever I needed to look at the horizon. Dismissing my fears, I stuff crackers and cookies into my pockets, grab my camera from my room and head up to the bridge.

From my new vantage point I can see how the sea rages. I focus my camera on every window and take my shots.

Water and glass. Instruments and charts. There's some relief found in this impersonal, detached view of the storm.

The captain shoots me a reassuring smile but he's sweating and looks pale which only makes me feel worse. I decide to return to my room, far from the sight of nervous captains, walls of green water, waves crashing violently on the deck. I'm halfway to my destination when the hulking tanker gives one of its huge shudders. The snap that sounds this time makes an other-worldly noise akin to the low, guttural groan of a Tibetan monk chanting. The entire ship shakes from bow to stern. This time the rumble is so ferocious I fall to my knees in the passageway and wait there until I can stand up again.

I take a deep breath, gather myself and find the strength to grope my way back to my quarters. Maybe sleep will help—if I can sleep at all with this commotion. I'm more exhausted than I've ever been in my life, but when I lie down sleep eludes me. I lie there, eyes wide open. An hour passes. Pete's story of the diesel generator blowing rolls through my head. I stretch and glance at my enemy: the clock. If I could only get comfortable. If the storm would just go away. I'm too exhausted to fight off the jagged thoughts. Fires. Waves. Explosions. I lie awake until after midnight, then I go to find Vanessa, who's on watch.

"I know you said you've never been really frightened, but have you been in other storms like this?" I ask when I find her.

"When the swells are this high, we just need to hit each wave at an angle. If we hit one of these mothers head on, it could suspend the ship in the middle. Break her back. So we angle the ship, then roll over it. That's all and we'll be fine."

"Are you sure?" I ask.

A few minutes later a tube fails in one of the two boilers. "It's common," she says sighing. "Tubes fail a lot, but this is bad timing." There's an edge to her voice I've never heard before. "When one fails, we have to shut down the boiler and cool it off for eighteen hours before we can get inside to work on it. We'll be running with only one boiler at sixty percent power for awhile."

As we're talking, one of the guy who's given Vanessa a hard time from day one, walks in. Vanessa is just about to open a valve, and he yells, "Stay away, we've had enough problems without a girl opening a valve half-assed and causing another emergency."

Then he pushes Vanessa. She shoves him right back and yells, "If you ever lay another hand on me the captain and every top dog in every union hall will hear about it." Then she adds, "Move over right now so I can open that valve."

As she speaks, I feel the tension growing. We're a tight-knit group of people with hidden animosities. It wouldn't take much to set someone off at this point.

"Look," I say, "we all know we can't accomplish all the tasks by ourselves and need to work as a team. I've been told that when there's an emergency, mariners put aside everything they don't like about someone. If it's them in trouble, they'll want someone else to help them out."

He mumbles, gets out of her way and leaves. I turn to Vanessa and laugh. "You're pretty tough for a girl."

"Remember to whom you are speaking!" She smiles. "Seriously, being down here is better than being up there in my room, alone. There's a comfort watching the other QMED's hustle and pull together in the hole. It's noisy and hot down here, but even though I'm surrounded by buckets clanging, alarms sounding and men yelling, it feels peaceful. No one should be alone in a storm."

"What would happen if the other boiler fails while this one's down?"

"We have to get it up and running as quickly as possible. We need all the power we can get to head into the storm. You can compare the tubes to the insides of an old tea kettle filled with build-up, except that the tubes get pitted on the outside and the inside, and a pitting on the outside can build up a hot spot that transfers to the inside. Tube failures always happen by the build-up on the inside of the tube, so the water has to be very pure in the boilers in order to prevent scale and other things that cause hot spots."

When Vanessa hasn't answered my question, I ask again. "What would happen if we lost both boilers at the same time?"

She takes a deep breath. "If we lose the fires in both boilers at the same time, we lose way, then steerage. If we lose the power in this mother, we won't stay bow into it and we'll turn broadside. In a storm like this, especially if the seas get much bigger, even this eight hundred foot tanker could roll over like a puppy if it got broadside to the waves."

We stare at each other, listening to the moaning of the ship.

On Vanessa's watch, a few more serious problems occur—flooding in other areas. We come through each of them one by one, because the ship is sectioned off so that if one area floods, we can secure the area. It might flood solid, but we still won't lose the buoyancy of the ship to the point it would sink. "We're floating," she says.

"That's what we want, right?" I say. She nods.

When her watch is over, we go back to her room and sit side-by-side on her bunk, because even though she has tied the chair to her desk with a long line, it's sliding too much to sit on it.

"How do you fall asleep with all this?" I ask, shaking my head.

"I'm always on call, but when I do sleep, it's the sleep of the dead. My alarm doesn't even wake me up. The first engineer says I better figure out a way to get down there when they need me. So I'm thinking about sleeping in the enclosed control room behind the console in the engine room. That way, someone can yell right in my ear when they need me."

Suddenly, the ship takes a big roll. I fall off the bunk, land under the desk and catch myself with my sore hands. I'm under the desk trying to hide the pain when Vanessa kneels beside me, takes my swollen hands in hers. "I wouldn't be on this ship still if it weren't for you. You've inspired us so much with your upbeat, can-do, caring attitude and determination to succeed," she says gently. "Especially me. You've given me strength I thought I'd lost.

"Maybe it's not strength but stubbornness," I say. "Anyway, all I've done is listen."

She shushes me in her Texas accent. "In a fearful time, that can be the most important thing."

She places the palms of her hands together as if in prayer, then makes the sign of the cross over my hands. "Anyway, don't let this be your major memory of what shipping is about." She looks at me and smiles. "It's beautiful places to see and wonderful people to meet. Come on, Jeanne. We're gonna have a slumber party. It's rolling too much to sleep in our bunks."

Vanessa hauls her mattress, blankets and pillow down onto the deck of her room. Next thing I know, she's got my mattress and bedding in there too. She arranges our mattresses at a ninety degree angle, our pillows head-to-head. I go back to my room, brush my teeth and change into my pajamas. When I return to Vanessa's room, she too is ready for bed.

"This is a girl's slumber party. No boys allowed," she says, handing me two Motrin for the pain in my hands. I slurp them down with some water, then climb into the makeshift bed she's made us.

Vanessa climbs under her own covers. "What's the first thing you want to do when you get home?" she asks, trying to get my mind off the storm.

"Call my daughters and friends from home instead of from a pay phone," I say, love for my girls filling my heart and voice.

"Then what?"

"Then I'd soak in a hot bath while I eat dark chocolate and drink red wine. I'd enjoy the land where I can hear the ravens greet me in the morning, feed the chipmunks, smell fresh cut wood, swim in the river. How about you?" I ask.

"I want to save enough money to buy a house, my first house where I can live with my daughter. Then I want to start a small business."

Vanessa looks toward her porthole as if she can see the new house, the new work.

A few moments of silence pass between us.

"What's the worst storm you were ever in?" I ask.

"The first time I saw green water."

I nod. "The Captain gave me my first view of that stuff."

"Yeah, it's pretty scary."

Neither of us says anything for a minute or two. Occasionally Vanessa glances over at me to see how I'm doing.

I try to take a deep breath. The groaning sound rumbles from the bow of the ship, but somehow I feel stronger, safer now.

And like a child being told a bedtime story, I slowly, gently drift off to sleep.

A few hours later I awake to the clap of loud thunder. I find my way back to my own cabin, change my clothes and head down to the galley. Rich greets me at breakfast and teases me when I say I'm not hungry.

"Oh. So now you're on a diet, huh." He asks several times what food sounds good to me, says I look pale and skinny. "This is the first day you haven't had your regular. Scrambled with cheese," he says.

"Black tea. That's all I want. Tea."

Again there is an easy menu for breakfast and lunch. Both meals consist of grilled cheese sandwiches. But when we hit our biggest roll yet, the ship screams at the blast of the water and pots and pans crash to the deck. Amidst the clanging cookware, the sinks again emit a foul-smelling discharge. The scent clears the chow line just as fast as it did the other day.

Rich looks around the galley. "Well, that was one big roll. Yes sir."

"You alright Jeanne?" Figarino asks from the chow line. "Come up to the bridge again after lunch. See what's going on out there."

As soon as I finish cleaning the galley and the dishes, I cash in on the captain's offer. I need to see again with my own eyes what we're up against. Has anything changed since I took my photos yesterday? The captain greets me, motions me to follow him. "We're not going anywhere in this. Just maintaining direction. Come and take a look."

Forty-foot swells are fore and aft. *And we will be stalled here for exactly how long?* I want to ask. But the AB at the helm makes a strange noise and Figarino's face goes taut. Sweat is dripping from the captain's chin. I turn to look at what has caught their attention as the biggest wave I've ever seen crashes up and over the bow. We roll, roll way over to port side. Glowing white water covers the deck. A light shining up from somewhere makes the water on deck look like an electric milk bath. Maybe the back door to the pump shop has come open and it's the light from inside. Whatever the source, the upper deck is like a giant swimming pool at night with the light shining up through the water.

For a split second there's silence. My mind spins back.

I think about the time I almost drowned in the pool, about Dad teaching me to float. The present streaks back as the captain motions to me.

"Freak wave," Figarino says. "Not to worry."

I nod my head not trusting myself to speak.

I return to my room frightened and I decide I want to write quick good-bye notes to my daughters and to my friends Elizabeth and Paul just in case the worst occurs.

My Dear Emily and Lisa,

The storm is huge and frightening. I have faith we'll make it but if we don't I want to say good-bye.

I'm sorry I'll miss all the exciting moments that will be happening in your lives. You've taught me much about love. I know you'll follow your hearts to all the right places. You were both always smarter than your mom. Thank you for the privilege of being your mother and friend.

I love you forever,

Mom

Dear Elizabeth and Paul,

If I never see you again, please know that the two of you have been a safe haven for me, a constant when everything else was in flux. I want you to know that something has shifted for me out here. All my life people have told me that I'm a strong person, but I never believed them. Now I know that it's true.

I hope we make it home. There's so much I haven't done yet.

I love you both,

Jeanne

I place the letters inside the mini refrigerator and seal it tight with duct tape, hoping the tape will keep the fridge tightly closed until the ship is found. Then I force myself to put thoughts of not making it out of my mind.

I go back to the crew mess. Stanley's there, drinking a cup of coffee. I notice his hands shaking.

"How ya doing?" he asks.

"Good, I think, and you?"

"Yep," he says, slurping.

I put my hand on his shoulder. "Stanley, are you scared?"

"Oh, not so much. Not so much, kiddo."

"Tell me something that will make me laugh," I say.

"You're the funny one," he says.

I know that talking will help him steady his nerves. I urge him to start. "You first."

He glances up at the bulkhead, then checks his watch. "Okay. You ever hear the one about Sven, Oly and Lena?" he slowly begins.

I shake my head.

"Well, Lena enters a swimming contest in the breast stroke category, and when she comes in last, she drags herself out of the water, discouraged and a little upset. Lena says to Sven, 'Ooh, say. Ya know, some of them other gals was using their arms.'"

I laugh.

Stanley's eyes fill. He sets his cup down on the table. "I am off to work overtime, Jeanne."

Left alone there, my thoughts turn to my father and old feelings of anger, caught in this life-death storm, somehow are beginning to change.

I'm sitting across from Dad. Still big as dinner plates, his hands shake while he stirs a cup of coffee. He sits with his legs crossed, leans to one side and without a greeting says how sorry he is that he wasn't a better father to me, that he felt powerless and reached to me for comfort.

His head starts shaking too when he says he didn't mean to hurt me, just to make himself feel better.

"I loved you, but I know I wasn't much of a father." He doesn't cry outwardly with tears streaming down his face. He cries inside; the kind of crying that twists his guts. Then he's gone.

I have made the conscious choice to forgive my dad but the missing piece has been my inability to feel compassion for him.

Now the thought of possibly dying in this ocean storm brings about that peace of mind I've been missing. Finally I see him as a tortured human being. I know I faced one of the scariest things a person can face as a child—abuse by a parent—and I survived.

Because of these experiences I realize at this moment, facing the storm, that in the past I've been on a death path, barely staying alive. Now I want to put the past in its place. It is then that I know the truth. The most fearful part of being in this storm is not what's happening outside, but the involuntary opening up of my heart. As frightening as it feels when this is happening, anything seems possible. Even forgiveness. Even fulfillment.

Just as my thoughts come together, Vanessa walks into the crew mess, taps me on the shoulder. "You okay, Jeanne? You look like you're in a daze," she says. She flashes me a smile and I see relief on her face. I realize she's been worried, too. "Storm's taken a turn for the better. Winds are settling down. We'll be moving forward soon and you'll be off this old heap before you know it."

I smile back and glance at the clock. Time to set up for dinner. It's been a long siege, one filled with tempestuous thoughts, a ferocious storm, a resolution of past turbulence and, most of all, the rebirth of my desire to live—really live.

Chapter Fifteen

Strangers on Shore

Just as we glide back to normal and the ship moves toward its destination, Captain Figarino receives a call that his father is dying. He gets off in Bellingham a day ahead of schedule in order to be with his dad in Baltimore. I don't get to say good-bye. He's gone before most of us realize it.

Periodically, I look out the passageway window facing the bow to see if the gangplank is in place. I want to call my daughters and then Elizabeth and tell them I'll be home tomorrow.

After dinner, Dave's in the crew lounge watching a movie as I leave for shore. He's sprawled out on the longest

sofa wearing baggy plaid shorts and red flip flops. He smiles
and waves when he sees me.

"Have fun tonight," he says. "And Jeanne?"

"Yeah?"

"Sleep in tomorrow morning."

"Sleep in?"

"Yeah. It's your last day. I'll cover for you down here.
If it gets too hectic, I'll knock on your door."

"What about the rooms?"

"Don't worry about rooms on your last day."

"Sleep in. What a concept. Thanks."

It's light when Rich pounds on my door at 5:30. "Coming to
work this morning?" He's a slave to routine.

My replacement shows up in time to help with
lunch. I show him around the ship, explaining clearly and in
more detail than was explained to me, his duties as steward
assistant. Lastly, I walk out to the phones to call the airlines.
I'm going home.

The new captain is sitting at his desk when I knock promptly
at 11:45.

"Come in. Come in," he says.

"Morning, sir. Sorry we won't be able to work together.
I've heard good things about you," I say.

"Well, don't believe any of it," he says, and, handing me a baseball cap with the merchant marine emblem, he wishes me luck. I feel like a real mariner when I sign off, my name forever written in the ship's log, stating when I got on and off the O.S. Illinois.

I turn to go and the captain says, "Aren't you forgetting something?" He hands me my paycheck—almost eight thousand dollars.

A gradual distancing begins once everyone knows I'll soon be leaving the ship. It's as if when one person goes ashore, everyone else becomes a stranger, as though the sea is the magical glue that holds us together and land just doesn't do the trick. I leave with mixed emotions. I won't miss the work, but I'll miss my new friends.

I walk down to the galley to say good-bye. Big Dave gives me a giant bear hug. "I'll help with your luggage when it's time," he says.

Rich is standing beside the two big ovens pretending that he's busy. I thank him for being a good boss. I thank him for everything, especially the laughs, then extend my hand. I'm almost crying. Rich is trying to smile but not doing a good job of it. He carefully shakes my extended hand. Then he gets all efficient, picks up a towel, swats it loud against the stove. "Salads to make, veggies to chop. Busy, busy, busy," he says. Then he turns, waves a brisk good-bye.

Robby's in the passageway wearing his orange coveralls. I stand immobile, unable to meet him even half way. Next to Vanessa, this is perhaps the most difficult farewell of all. He hugs me tenderly, kisses me on the cheek, then, with a hand on each of my shoulders, studies my face. There are tears and compassion in his dark brown eyes.

"Bye, Jeanne. Remember your promise to go back to teaching," he says.

I laugh. Then we're silent. We stare at each other for a second before I turn to go.

I'm checking my room one last time to see if I have everything when someone knocks on my door. It's Kyle. He stands there all shy like, his amber hair hanging down on his forehead. Then, as if that isn't awkward enough, out walks Rich from his door to see what's afloat. Rich looks up at Kyle, then down at me.

"Oops. Thought the knock was on my door," he says and backs into his room.

I invite Kyle in. He's the first man to be in my room.

"It's been great having you on board," he says.

"Yeah. Me too, you," I say awkwardly.

"I'm sorry to see you leave." He reaches down, hugs me big. "I marked my favorite," he says, handing me back the copy of Neruda I lent him weeks and weeks ago.

"Thank you. Thank you for everything. I'll read it on the plane."

I carry my small duffel bag. Dave hauls the moose. We're walking toward the gangplank where Stanley and other ABs are busy at work. Stanley nods good-bye without words.

As I make my way down the gangplank, a wave of nausea sweeps over me. All I want to do is turn around right now, go back onto the tanker and lie on the bunk in my cabin for a while. Even being outside, I can't seem to get enough air in my lungs. I feel my chest tightening and all thoughts lead to one simple conclusion: I am going to miss the O.S. Illinois. Just as I'm reaching the end of the gangplank, I hear Vanessa screech my name. I'm trying to leave without seeing her, because I know it will be too hard for both of us. I've left her a note, but she's running on the deck to catch up with me. Running on deck is strictly forbidden, but she's running anyway. She reaches the gangplank and descends. I meet her half way with a hug. She hands me a card and a bright yellow pack of peanut M&Ms.

"I'm gonna miss you," she says.

"You're going to make it," I say.

"Yeah." She wipes her eyes.

Now I'm crying too. We're hugging and she's so much shorter than I am that I pat her on top of her head like I used to do when my daughters were small.

"Promise to call me," I say.

"Yeah, you bet I'll call you. I'll call anybody lucky enough to get off this hell-hole ship," she says.

"And promise me you won't go back with him."

"Jeanne, after he messed me up so bad this last time and I got away, I prayed. I said, 'Please. I need your help. I don't know what to do or where to go. Please send someone to help me.' And who's the first person I see when I get on this dip-shit flat-lander ship? You."

We hug one last time.

Halfway to the phones I turn back. Vanessa waves. She's standing on the deck a few feet from Stanley, who yells, "Bye kiddo. You made it!" He's waving, arm poised in mid-air. As I wait for the cab, I open up the book of Neruda's poetry and flip to the page Kyle marked. I begin to read his favorite poem:

Strangers on the Shore

I have come back, and still the sea
keeps sending me strange foam.
It does not get used to the way I see.
The sand does not recognize me.

There's more to the poem, but I stop. Rest. Close my eyes. The distance is real.

Chapter Sixteen

Home

I land in Portland, the city of two rivers, the Columbia and the Williamette. It's five o'clock and by 5:30 I'm on the street where I live. When the cab driver pulls in my driveway and I see my little bungalow with the lush green grass and red, yellow and orange sweet scented flowers in the yard, I'm overcome with gratitude. I can't believe the beauty of this earth; I'm overwhelmed by the colors and smells. This is my home.

I leave a message for my friend Elizabeth that I've returned and head out to the small convenience store for coffee, milk and cereal. When I get back to the house, I see that Elizabeth has been here. On my dining room table

beside a bottle of Merlot sits a bowl filled with fruit, chocolate cookies and brownies.

For a few seconds I wonder what I'll do without ten
toilets to clean, ten beds to make, four stories of stairs and
passageways to mop, sinks full of dirty dishes. Then I relax
with a crystal glass filled with the mellow, deep red merlot
which I sip slowly.

I sleep until nine something the next morning, and
after my first leisurely cup of coffee, I walk into the kitchen
for my second cup, open the kitchen blinds and spot
Elizabeth in my back yard, bundled up, on her hands and
knees, weeding. I open the back door and stand there in my
robe while she weeds.

"What do you think you're doing?" I ask.

"You know, I just love the sound of the birds in your
back yard," she says.

"What are you doing?" I ask again.

Now she rises and turns toward me. "I couldn't bear
the thought of you out here weeding with your sore hands."
Then she walks over, climbs my back steps and gives me a
hug.

Later I go to an acupuncturist for the pain in my hands.

He holds them up and says, "Poor little hands. You're
too small for work like that, aren't you." He looks at me and

says, "Never do work like that again. Work like that is for big six-foot, four-inch men named Olaf. Your body isn't made for that kind of work."

As he inserts needle after needle into my hands, I tell him that the needle causing the most pain is the one he inserts in the flesh between the ring and little finger of my left hand. "Jeanne, that is your heart meridian. Sometimes things happen to our bodies that express within our body what is happening in our lives. It can be pretty phenomenal."

Three days after I'm home, my father's health deteriorates and becomes critical. The phone call from the hospice nurse says he has a day or two to live. She says Dad's vitals are unstable, his breathing shallow.

"Can he talk on the phone?" I ask.

"I think it would hurt him too much to talk right now," she says.

"Can you give him a message from me when he wakes up?"

"Sure, hon."

"Tell him his daughter Jeanne called. Tell him I love him."

"Okay, darling."

"Do you think that will be too upsetting for him? We've been estranged a long time."

"No honey. It's a good thing."

"Thank you. Is he in a lot of pain?"

"We're keeping him as comfortable as possible. Call back in an hour. He'll be awake and you can talk with him."

I think about the good things I experienced as a child: the farm, the wheat fields, cattails, big oaks and mums beside the house. I think of Dad carrying me on his shoulders in the swimming pool. I dial a florist and order him a bouquet.

I speak with my older sister on the phone. She wants me to come out there but I feel my father's death should be a time of peace not confrontation. I don't want to bring negativity to his deathbed. I will say my good-byes from two thousand miles away.

But I vacillate from moment to moment about whether I've made the right decision. I want to be able to hold his hand, tell him in person that I love him despite all that happened. I call several airlines, a travel agent. I put tickets on hold, but I cannot bring myself to go. Something inside just holds me back.

I call my daughter Emily and tell her what's happening. "Mom, this is between you and your dad. You've communicated your love for him through the nurse and telepathically. He's hearing you. He's getting your messages. I think you know the best way to say good-bye."

My friend Elizabeth agrees. "I'm concerned that if you go out there, all the good healing you've now done will be undone by all the unsettled stuff," she says. "You've sent him love and forgiveness. He's heard you. Trust in this."

I choose to avoid a family drama at his bedside.

I call the hospice again. This time my younger sister picks up the phone. She says Dad is awake and can talk with me.

I overhear her say, "Dad, there's somebody here you haven't talked with in a long time. It's Jeanne. Do you want to talk with her?" She says he's nodding his head yes and smiling. She tells me that she's passing the phone to him. I hear him mumbling.

"Hi Dad. I hope you're comfortable. I hope you're not in too much pain, that it's not too hard on you."

He whispers into the phone. I can barely decipher every other word. "Jeanne...good to hear...yes."

"I love you," I say.

The hospice nurse gets back on the line. "He looks happy, hon. You should see his face."

I stare out the front window at the yellow leaves on the birch tree.

"He's been real peaceful since your first message, even more now with you talking with him."

"Tell him I love him. Tell him good-bye."

The October leaves rustle under my feet as I walk down to the Columbia River north of my home. I carry a basket filled with roses Elizabeth dried while I was at sea. Reds, yellows, pinks, peaches and whites. There's also pine cones and dried purple hydrangea from Paul. In my other hand I carry the last letter I'll write to Dad, tied with a ribbon.

I walk down a rock-lined path, pass an old stump with a rusted horseshoe, pause at the water's edge to take in the beauty of the sun, feel the loose sand beneath my feet, hear the sound of water lapping the shore.

It's mid-week, not crowded. I ease down onto a rock in a sheltered cove where I sit in silence. Distant boats drift through the afternoon. Dragonflies dart, fish nibble the water's surface and a blue heron disappears in a deep dive.

I put down the letter and bouquet, immediately thinking of the two sides of my father. The man who hurt me, because he was hurting inside, and the loving man who relished life when he wasn't in so much pain. I thank my dad for the loving parts of himself that he shared with me. I thank him for his whistling and singing when he worked in the barn. I thank him for his dancing after the card parties he and Mom hosted. I thank him and their friends for teaching me how to waltz, polka, fox-trot, one-step, two-step.

In the letter I tell him that I forgive him; as a fellow spirit I forgive him. Then I ask him to forgive me for the way I handled the confrontation years ago. I ask him to forgive me for the pain that my revelation of the truth caused him.

This is our good-bye, Dad. Forgiveness feels like birth. A divine birth. Thank you for the new life you've given me. We both live in the forgiveness.

Slowly, I sprinkle the basket's wealth on the water: letter, roses, pine cones and hydrangea float off to sea.

Chapter Seventeen

Reverie

At sea I ate, slept, drank and worked surrounded by steel, water and men. Six people allowed me brief glimpses into their lives and in them I saw a vulnerability beneath tough exteriors. I saw hearts similar to mine: tender, bruised and guarded. Still today, like loved ones, I carry them with me: Dave and Robby, the older and kid brothers; Rich, the uncle who let me work in his kitchen; Kyle, the would-be lover; Stanley, the eccentric but caring father; Vanessa, the spunky sister. Being a small part of their ship family helped me.

My self-worth no longer relies on my past script. I've shifted position, a complete shift of thought wherein I realize that the past does not define me.

When I found true compassion for my parents, I began to build a true story of myself. I quit waiting to be rescued, stepped into the breach, and saved myself. Bright, articulate, talented, powerful, I began breaking free. "The world has a great many sleep walkers," a friend once told me. It also has strange ways of waking us.

As soon as I got to Portland, I began decorating my house to suit the new me. I transformed the second bedroom into my private space for reflection, reading and writing. Textured Turkish rugs and pillows, rich paintings on three walls, a quilt symbolizing new life on the fourth—this is where I write. Photos of Emily and Lisa, Elizabeth and Paul, look back at me from the desktop.

Next came the art space. Six contractors said the falling-down, hole-in-the-roof, tilted garage could not be fixed. The seventh, a country boy whose father straightened old barns, talked my language. He salvaged the foundation and center wall, brought in pulleys and had the structure straight in no time. We used the interior tongue-in-groove cedar siding for the floor in what is now my vaulted ceiling, bright art studio with a sky light. It's two-hundred-fifty square feet of bliss.

Argentine tango, my newest dance form, has become my way to express the Sergei within.

The two-year hiatus I took from dating after I returned to land has made me wiser and more selective. I see more clearly who people really are.

I support myself doing odd jobs, some more unique than others. Sometimes I'm a film extra. Sometimes I teach. I sell my paintings when a new series pleases me. Odd jobs add variety to my life.

I think that moving to Portland was providential. The rainy city where powerful rivers converge.

One morning a few weeks ago, I sat in my kitchen drinking coffee and dreaming up a flower garden for my backyard, when my old pal Fred York called. He told me the O.S. Illinois had just survived a truly savage storm. This time, five million dollars worth of damage had been done, and she would need months of repairs in dry dock. I thought about my former home, the old rust bucket as I drew an imaginary curving gravel walkway through the beds of English lavender just to the right of the purple smoke tree I'll plant near my back door.

True to the tattoo dream I had before going to sea, my hands are forever marked: one with an emblem of courage, the other with the rose of an open heart. I returned home with hand injuries that required surgery and intensive physical therapy. The wounds are healing. I paint. I write.

The sea has changed the course of my life. In the confines of that small drab room on board, I shed my old snake skin. Now, I walk out the kitchen sliding door twenty steps past lavender and catmint, and into my studio to finish

a new canvas. I'll work till the light fails, then lie awake to
watch the moon travel the sky from east to west.

Glossary

AB or able-bodied seaman: an experienced member of the deck department who reports to the mates and performs routine deck maintenance and assists on the bridge

bridge: the forward part of a ship's super structure from which the ship is navigated

boatswain or bosun: a petty officer on a merchant ship in charge of the deck crew and hull maintenance

captain: an officer who is master or commander of a ship, head of the deck department and responsible for the navigation of the ship *chief cook:* a crew member who works in the steward department and is responsible for meal preparation

chief engineer: an officer and engineer who is head of and responsible for managing the engine department

DEU or deck engine utility: a crew member who works in all three departments: deck, engine and utility

deck: a platform on a ship which serves as a structural element and forms the floor of the ship's compartments

engineer: an officer in the engine department who reports to the chief engineer and supervises the operation of the engines

deck hand: see AB or able-bodied seaman

galley: the kitchen of a ship

GSU or general steward utility: a crew member who works in the steward department and assists in the galley with setup and clean up of meals and is responsible for cleaning officers' rooms as well as the upper section of the house

hole, the: the engine room(s) in the lower decks of a ship

launch: a small boat that carries crew members and quantities of supplies to and from the ship *mate:* an officer in the deck department who ranks below the captain and is responsible for navigation of the ship

merchant marine: the privately or publicly owned commercial ships of a nation; the personnel of a merchant marine

pilot: one employed to steer a ship during voyage; person who is specially qualified and usually licensed to conduct a ship into and out of a port or in specified waters

port side: the left side of a ship looking forward

QMED or qualified man in the engine department: a crew member who works in the engine department and reports to the engineers

SA or steward assistant: see GSU or general steward utility

smudge: a Native American custom of burning sweet grass or sage in order to cleanse a person of negative energy

starboard: the right side of a ship looking forward

stern: the rear most portion of a ship

chief steward: a crew member in charge of the steward department who manages the provisioning of food, the preparation of all meals and supervises the chief cook and steward assistant

tanker: a cargo ship fitted with large tanks for carrying liquid in bulk

Z Card: a required identification card for members of the merchant marines